FOREWORD

Family law is a continuously growing subject. There is a steady stream of important case-law. Parliament passes at least one major family law Act each year. Practice directions have a major impact on the conduct of cases. Government departments issue guidance by official circulars. Influential articles appear in the legal press.

It is desperately hard for the busy practitioner to keep up to date. He needs first to be able to identify the legal issues involved in his clients' problems and then to be able to find the answers to them as quickly as possible. The aim of this 'Guide and Practice' Series is to help him to do both.

The books in the Series are written by recognized experts – some primarily academics and some primarily practitioners, but all with an insight into the realities of family law. They set out to answer the problems and queries which busy practitioners are likely to face. But that does not mean that the books are superficial. Our philosophy is that the practitioner deserves and needs the highest standards of specialist legal scholarship; and the authors all bring a wide and deep knowledge of their subject to their task.

Stephen Cretney

GUIDE AND PRACTICE SERIES

GENERAL EDITOR: PROFESSOR STEPHEN CRETNEY

Published by
Jordan & Sons Limited
21 St. Thomas Street, Bristol BS1 6JS

Copyright © 1988 Jordan & Sons Limited

1st Edition 1986
2nd Edition 1988

ISBN 0 85308 112 3 ✓

Typeset and printed by The Eastern Press,
Reading and London

PREFACE TO THE
SECOND EDITION

This book is written primarily for legal practitioners, and our purpose is to give them a clear and practical account of child-care law. Much has happened since the first edition appeared two years ago. Child sexual abuse has received much publicity, a new set of Children and Young Persons Rules has been passed implementing the Children and Young Persons (Amendment) Act 1986, and there has been a marked increase in the number of reported child-care cases. These and other developments appear throughout the book but the most significant changes from the first edition appear in chapters 1, 4, 6 and 7. The structure of the book is as follows. There are certain evidential and preparatory matters which pose particular problems in child-care proceedings and these are explored and explained in chapter 1. Chapter 2 covers the reception of children into care under the 1980 Act, the assumption of parental rights, and the court proceedings which may follow. Chapter 3 describes the grounds for care proceedings under the 1969 Act, and chapter 4 the hearing before the juvenile court. Here both the new Rules and case-law have led to important revisions, in particular a much expanded discussion of interim orders. The way in which parents may seek access to children in care is explained in chapter 5. The availability and role of wardship and other remedies are discussed in chapter 6. We focus particular attention on the expanding role of judicial review in the child-care context. Finally, chapter 7 focuses on the special difficulties encountered by third parties, such as grandparents, natural fathers and foster-parents, in obtaining a hearing within the statutory framework.

The law is examined both from the point of view of the lawyer advising a local authority and from that of his counterpart who is advising the child or his parents. We attempt to highlight problems which are likely to arise in practice and suggest the means by which they can be resolved. Where the law is unclear we venture to suggest particular solutions. We hope this book will be of value not only to practitioners and justices' clerks but also to social workers and other

professionals concerned with children in care, for wherever possible
we seek to identify the social policy underlining the legal framework.
Those who are engaged in law reform may also find this book helpful
when considering the adequacy of the present legal structure.

We owe special thanks to Graham Battersby, Hugh Bevan and
Catherine Williams who each read drafts of the first edition and made
many helpful suggestions. Jean Hopewell, who typed the manuscript
of both editions with great skill and patience, is owed a particular
debt of gratitude. Mary Hayes would also like to thank her husband
and three older children for their support and encouragement. Her
part in this book is dedicated to her two small daughters, Rosemary
and Jennifer.

The law is stated as at 8 September 1988.

Mary Hayes
Vaughan Bevan

CONTENTS

TABLE OF CASES

TABLE OF STATUTES

TABLE OF STATUTORY INSTRUMENTS

TABLE OF RULES

1 EVIDENCE

1.1 Child-Care Cases

Children come into local authority care by various routes. Sometimes it is as a result of a court order made in care, guardianship, matrimonial or wardship proceedings. In other cases the entry into care is voluntary, but may be turned into compulsory care by an administrative resolution which can then be challenged in a court. Where access to a child in care is refused or terminated this too can be litigated. The child, the parents, and the local authority all have an interest in the outcome of the proceedings, and occasionally others have a right to be heard by the court. Consequently, several lawyers can be involved in the preparation and presentation of a case and the difficulties facing them will vary.

1.2 The Juvenile Court

Most child-care proceedings are heard in the juvenile court. Its procedures are regulated by the Magistrates' Courts (Children and Young Persons) Rules 1988 (CYP Rules 1988); and hearings before it are governed by the normal rules of evidence. But at the outset it should be noted that in civil cases the court retains some discretion on how to conduct its proceedings, and this can temper the rigour of the procedural and evidential rules. For example, care proceedings are normally conducted in two stages, and proof of grounds for intervention must be established before reports are admissible to assist the court in determining what order to make (see §4.5). However, where all parties and others with a right to be heard in the case agree that an order should be made, the court may be asked to read the guardian ad litem's report and the social inquiry report before the application commences. The CYP Rules 1988 make no allowance for this approach, but it can be eminently sensible and is followed in practice.

It has been held that a juvenile court can conduct its proceedings with flexibility where this promotes the interests of justice. Thus, in

1

R v *Gravesham Juvenile Court ex parte B* (1983) 4 FLR 312 it was held that this principle enabled a court to allow parents to be legally represented in care proceedings; and in *R* v *Milton Keynes Justices ex parte R* [1979] 1 WLR 1062 it entitled the court to allow parents to cross-examine witnesses. While both of these decisions have to a large extent been overtaken by changes in legislation and the rules (see §4.2), they could none the less prove useful precedents should an analogous situation occur. For example, third parties are sometimes entitled under the rules to make representations to the court (see §7.5.3) and arguably the court could allow them to be legally represented if this would serve the interests of justice.

Clearly, there must be a limit to the proper exercise of the court's discretion, and the broad statements by Lord Widgery CJ in *Humberside CC* v *DPR* [1977] 1 WLR 1251, that care proceedings are essentially 'non-party' and 'non-adversarial', must be treated with caution for, where there is a direct conflict with the rules of procedure and evidence, the rules must prevail. Nevertheless in the *Humberside* case it was partly in reliance on this approach that the Divisional Court ruled that hearsay evidence was admissible (an alternative ground for its admissibility is explained in §1.3.6). Furthermore, in *R* v *Wood Green Crown Court ex parte P* (1983) 4 FLR 206 the court objected to technical points of evidence being raised. Thus, the lawyer in the juvenile court will frequently find that he must strike a balance between allowing breaches of the rules of evidence and procedure to pass without comment (a common example is the recounting of hearsay information by an inexperienced witness) and objecting to such breaches when they damage the interests of his client. Against this background a crucial factor for the lawyer is an understanding of how the local bench of magistrates operates and of the types of advice they are likely to receive from their clerks. Also, since the justices' clerk is empowered to perform judicial functions, liaison with clerks and an understanding of their practice are essential.

1.3 Evidence

When preparing a case the practitioner may find the following checklist helpful:

(1) what has to be proved and upon what standard of proof;
(2) who can or ought to give evidence;
(3) whether expert witnesses are needed;

(4) what types of evidence can or cannot be admitted or must be corroborated;

(5) whether there is some evidence which should not, or cannot in law, be disclosed to other parties and persons.

One preliminary point should be noted in respect of the role of the local authority's solicitor. The proper resolution of child-care cases requires good co-operation between a variety of agencies such as the Social Services Department, the health service and the police. This in turn entails the fullest and most accurate records of conversations and correspondence. The all too frequent reports into the deaths of abused children testify to the dangers of mislaid or ambiguously worded documentation. For the local authority these dangers are exacerbated by the workload on social services departments and the regular changeover in staff. A partial answer is the involvement of a vigilant and energetic lawyer at an early stage (perhaps by attending case conferences), who then rigorously collects and analyses the evidence.

1.3.1 Standard of proof

The juvenile court must be satisfied on a balance of probabilities that the applicant has discharged the burden of proving his case. The contrast with the criminal standard of proof beyond reasonable doubt is complex for, in a number of cases in other branches of law, the courts have decided that the requisite degree of probability in civil proceedings can vary according to the gravity of the issue to be resolved and of the consequences which can follow if it is proved; see *R* v *Secretary of State for the Home Department ex parte Khawaja* [1984] AC 74; *R* v *Milk Marketing Board ex parte Austin* (1983) *The Times*, March 21; *Re JS (A Minor)* (1981) 2 FLR 146; *W* v *K (Proof of Paternity)* [1988] 1 FLR 86.

The position in the child-care field has not yet been clarified but the logic of the cases (above) suggests that the standard is a high one. Since the transfer of parental rights is obviously a grave matter and since the Children and Young Persons Act 1969 (CYPA) and the Child Care Act 1980 (CCA) pay so much attention to the fitness or otherwise of the parent (proceedings can easily assume a gladiatorial air with the parents 'on trial'), then it can be argued by the parent that the court should demand something more than a mere balance of probabilities. However, it will be appreciated that there is a considerable forensic difference between persuading a bench, on the one hand that it is 'more probable than not' that a parent is unfit to care for a child, and on the other that 'there is a high degree of probability or near certainty' that this is so. Certainly the lower standard of a balance of probabilities has been approved in wardship proceedings (see *I* v *Barnsley MBC* [1986] 1 FLR 109; *Re R (A Minor)* [1988] 1 FLR 206), but the position was made more complex in *Re G (No. 2) (A Minor)* [1988] 1 FLR 314, which concerned sexual abuse. There Sheldon J suggested that a higher degree of probability is needed to satisfy a court that an individual (the father in that case) has sexually abused a child than that required merely to establish that the child has been sexually abused. It is suggested that any attempt to persuade a court to adopt the higher standard in child-care cases should be firmly resisted. An eyewitness account of how a child came to suffer an injury, or to develop symptoms of impaired development or neglect, is unusual. Opinion evidence from an expert witness is often an essential element in the case. Although experts are rarely able to state with certainty how a child's condition has come about, the expert's skill and experience will usually enable him to identify with confidence the cause of the child's condition on the balance of probabilities. The operation of a 'near certainty' standard could dissuade an authority from instituting proceedings in a proper case, or cause such an application to fail for lack of proof, and thus put a child's health and safety at risk. As to whether different standards should be applied to proof of abuse and identification of the abuser, it is suggested that any tendency to treat civil care proceedings as quasi-criminal should also be resisted. For, after abuse has been proved, work must be done with the child either to rehabilitate him with his family or to reconcile him with having been abused by a named perpetrator. Such work is liable to be frustrated if the perpetrator cannot be identified in civil proceedings.

1.3.2 Competence of witnesses

All persons are competent as witnesses, Evidence Act 1851, s. 2; Evidence Amendment Act 1853, s. 1, unless mental illness or infancy prevents them from giving evidence. The key to these disqualifications is whether the person is able to understand the nature and obligations of the oath. If there is a doubt, it is for the court to test the person's understanding and intelligence (cf. *R* v *Bird* (1988) *The Times*, June 22). This is of particular relevance of course to the evidence of children, for, unlike in criminal proceedings, there is no provision for the reception of unsworn evidence. A number of situations need to be distinguished. In care proceedings the child is always a party and he must attend the first and final hearings (unless he is under the age of five and the court agrees to his absence). Attendance at successive interim hearings is not essential, see *Northamptonshire CC* v *H* [1988] 2 WLR 389 and §4.3. In other proceedings, such as an access hearing, the child may be made a party. In that case his attendance is not necessary when he is legally represented. Clearly, the older a child is, the more likely it is that his advocate will advise him to attend. In those proceedings where the child is not made a party, he may be called as a witness by one of the parties, for example, if he has strong feelings on the issue of access. It is then that his competence to give evidence can particularly arise. Another example is where a child is called by the local authority to support a parental rights resolution passed because of his parent's alleged unfitness, CCA 1980, s. 3 (1) (*b*) (iv) and (v). In such situations the court must be satisfied of the child's competence and, in cases of doubt, must undertake the difficult, if not unreal, task of examining the child to see if he understands the seriousness of the occasion and the grave duty to tell the truth which the oath requires, *R* v *Campbell* [1983] Crim. LR 174. There is no age requirement for a child to satisfy the test. It has been suggested by the Court of Appeal in criminal proceedings that a rough guideline is the eight to ten-year-old age group, *R* v *Hayes* [1977] 1 WLR 234, whereas fourteen was the threshold suggested in *R* v *Khan* (1981) 73 Cr AR 190. All will depend upon the particular child's intelligence and maturity. There will be few occasions when a party will wish to call a child as a witness. Quite apart from the issue of competence, a child's sworn evidence still has to be treated with caution, problems of corroboration may arise (see §1.5), and the atmosphere of the courtroom may well reduce the child to silence or incoherence.

1.3.3 Expert witnesses

An important matter to be considered in the preparation of a case is whether reports and testimony from expert witnesses are needed. Apart from his special skill, an expert witness, unlike other witnesses, has the advantage that he is allowed to give opinion evidence based on his expertise. This is especially important in the difficult area of child sexual abuse. Who is an expert is a matter for the court to decide and a witness's status as an expert can be challenged by another party to the proceedings. Examples are a paediatrician, child psychiatrist, educational psychologist and health visitor. A social worker can give evidence about local social work practice, but if a particular aspect of child care such as the identification of an act of child abuse is in issue, the court must be satisfied that the social worker has the necessary skills and experience to speak as an expert witness on that aspect. The use of independent social workers in matrimonial and wardship proceedings has been discouraged, and in the juvenile court their employment is also infrequent, since the guardian ad litem's evidence and report and the local authority's social inquiry report will normally be sufficient guides for the court (and in *R* v *Sunderland Juvenile Court ex parte G* [1988] 2 FLR 40 the term 'independent' has been deprecated).

1.3.4 Guardian ad litem

When a guardian ad litem is appointed to safeguard and represent the interests of the child before the court, he is selected from a panel drawn up by the local authority under the Guardians ad Litem and Reporting Officers (Panels) Regulations 1983. He cannot be someone who is employed by, or connected with, the local authority or voluntary organization which are already a party to the proceedings. Full-time probation officers are excluded from being guardians ad litem, but part-time probation officers may be appointed, provided that they undertake this work in their own time and not as part of their official duties. A probation officer who has had prior involvement with the child or his family may not be appointed. The guardian ad litem's duties and powers are specified in the CYP Rules 1988, rr. 16 and 31; also, the DHSS has prepared a guide entitled *Guide for Guardians ad Litem*. For further discussion of his functions, see §4.1.1.

The guardian ad litem has a duty to inspect such records as he thinks appropriate. However, this does not give him a general right of access to these records and he may be met with claims of legal privilege, public interest immunity and confidentiality (see §1.6). In view of the guardian ad litem's status as an officer of the court it will be most unusual for a local authority or other agency to deny him access to material relevant to his enquiries and the preparation of his report. But where this does occur he can either report the obstruction back to the court for its advice or instruct the child's solicitor to issue a witness summons under the Magistrates' Courts Act 1980 (MCA), s. 97. This secures the attendance of any witness; the witness can be told to bring a particular document with him and the court will decide whether access to the information is justified. If the guardian ad litem believes that he is being seriously impeded in the performance of his functions, the solicitor should carefully consider whether to invoke judicial review. For it may be more appropriate for a judge of the High Court to determine whether documents are immune from disclosure to parties to the proceedings.

The guardian ad litem's report can only be handed to persons other than the parties or their legal advisers with the approval of the court (see *R* v *Sunderland Juvenile Court ex parte G* at §.4.2.2.). Practice varies. Many courts ask that its contents should be disclosed to the parties and parents in advance of the hearing, so that instructions can be given in response to it. In others, disclosure takes place at the hearing. Clearly, it is in the interests of all concerned that the former practice is followed, see *R* v *West Malling Juvenile Court ex parte K* [1986] 2 FLR 405; *R* v *Epsom Juvenile Court ex parte G* [1988] 1 All ER 329, and §4.5.1.

1.3.5 Compellability

In civil proceedings dealt with in this book all competent persons are compellable as witnesses. This is important in the child-care context because it means that one spouse can be compelled to attend as a witness to rebut the evidence of the other. For example, a mother can be called to support the local authority's complaint of child abuse made against the father. Moreover, there is no privilege against revealing communications between spouses so that one spouse can be freely cross-examined about conversations with the other, Civil Evidence Act 1968 (CEA), s. 16 (3). The possibility, however, of connivance between spouses will often reduce the usefulness of a spouse's evidence.

If a witness refuses to attend the court or to produce a document which he is legally obliged to deliver up, powers of compulsion are available, whereby a summons for attendance and, if necessary, a warrant for arrest can be issued, MCA 1980, s. 97. In care proceedings a warrant can be issued to secure the attendance of the child, CYPA 1969, s. 2 (4).

1.3.6 Hearsay

Part I of the CEA 1968, which admits certain kinds of hearsay evidence, has not been implemented in magistrates' courts and, it would appear, does not apply when appeals are taken to the Crown Court, see *R* v *Wood Green Crown Court ex parte P* (1983) 4 FLR 206. This means that the common-law rule against hearsay operates and that a witness can only testify to matters within his personal knowledge. Thus, in *Re S* (1980) 1 FLR 301 the mother made allegations against the father outside the court and refused to repeat them at the hearing. It was held that evidence of what she had alleged could not be related by a third party. Similarly, the comments of a neighbour or schoolteacher addressed, for example, to the social worker or guardian ad litem are inadmissible.

In *Humberside CC* v *DPR* [1977] 1 WLR 1251 the Lord Chief Justice permitted some amelioration of this common-law rule. He was prepared to admit in care proceedings statements made by a child's 'guardian' (as broadly defined by the Children and Young Persons Acts of 1933 and 1969, see §7.5.2) to a social worker, health visitor, police officer and NSPCC inspector in which the 'guardian' admitted to ill-treatment of the child. It may be that this case entitles a juvenile court to adopt a more relaxed attitude towards hearsay evidence in care proceedings, and in practice courts do allow some hearsay statements, whether intentionally or not. This approach (endorsed in the Scottish context by *W and Another* v *Kennedy* (1988) *The Times*, February 8) is encouraging from a local authority's point of view and will frequently be in the child's best interests but, if justice is to be done to all, there must be limits and it is suggested that a court should be slow to extend this first amelioration of the hearsay rule to issues which amount to serious allegations against a person (cf. the position in custody cases where hearsay relating to non-controversial matters may be admitted, but not if it relates to contentious matters, see *Thompson* v *Thompson* [1986] 1 FLR 212).

It is suggested, however, that the *Humberside* case is merely an amplification of a second amelioration to the hearsay rule, namely the common-law exception whereby the court will receive an admission or confession by a party to the proceedings, extended by the *Humberside* case, to include 'someone who has the control of the child or is concerned with the control of the child' (Lord Widgery CJ). This common-law exception to the rule against hearsay can be extremely valuable to the local authority. An admission by a parent to the police or a health visitor, for example, can be the decisive evidence in child-related proceedings. More importantly, in care proceedings the child is technically a party to the proceedings. Therefore statements made by the child to, for example, a doctor, nurse or school teacher can fall within this exception. However, the *Humberside* decision appears to have been confined in its scope by *Re S* (see above), so that a child's statement to a social worker that she is being sexually abused is admissible, whereas the statement that her father is the culprit is probably inadmissible. In practice such distinctions would prevent the court from properly exercising its judicial function of enquiring into the condition of the child and how this has come about (*Humberside*). Accordingly it is suggested that the court should adopt a more relaxed approach to the hearsay rule, admit both statements and recognise the hearsay nature of the evidence when assessing how much weight should be attached to it. Another approach is to admit the statements simply in order to prove that they were in fact made, and not in order to assert the truth of the facts alleged. If either approach were to be appealed, the superior courts would have an opportunity to clarify this uncertain area of the law. A third amelioration is the limited application of the Evidence Act 1938 (EA), by virtue of which very limited hearsay evidence is admissible in documentary form (see §1.4).

A further point to note in qualification to the hearsay rule is that in care proceedings under the CYPA 1969 there are two stages to the proceedings. First there must be proof of one of the grounds under s. 1, and then there is an assessment by the court of what order it should make (reports stage). The strict rules of evidence only apply to the first stage. This means that, at the second stage, a welfare report or report of a guardian ad litem can contain hearsay allegations and opinions. This twofold structure of care proceedings can cause confusion amongst parties and witnesses, quite apart from leading to some overlapping of evidence, and the lawyer should be careful to distinguish the two stages during preparation of the case. Moreover, the relaxation of the law at the reports stage should not be interpreted as an excuse for including every item of hearsay evidence, for otherwise the weight of the report may be challenged and may run the risk of being devalued in the eyes of the court.

Finally, it should be remembered that Part I of the CEA 1968 (which relaxes the rule against hearsay) applies to proceedings commenced in the higher courts. Quite apart from the Act's availability, the Family Division of the High Court adopts a lenient attitude to hearsay and such evidence will normally be admitted whenever the court feels that it may be relevant, see *Re N (Minors)* [1987] 1 FLR 65; *Re K* [1965] AC 201.

1.4 Documentary Evidence

There are a few occasions when the juvenile court is considering the merits of care and related proceedings when documentary evidence can be admitted at the proof stage. Although Part I of the CEA 1968 does not apply to magistrates' courts, the narrow terms of s. 1 of the Evidence Act 1938 do. Thus, a statement of facts in a document is admissible provided that, first, the maker of the statement has personal knowledge of those facts; secondly, he is called as a witness in the proceedings (or cannot be called because of death, illness, travel overseas, or unknown whereabouts); and, thirdly, he is not a person 'interested' in the proceedings. In this way reports by, for example, a health visitor, doctor and schoolteacher can be submitted for the court to read in advance of the witness giving his evidence. The witness can also use the report to refresh his memory and counsel can use it as a basis for cross-examination. It is at this point that problems of hearsay can be acute, for it can easily creep into a statement which is admitted under the EA 1938. For example, a consultant paediatrician may include in his statement evidence of a child's growth rate, including measurements prepared by his junior colleagues who are not called as witnesses. Whether such evidence can be presented depends largely on the forbearance of the court and the co-operation of the parties in overlooking technical infringements of the hearsay rule.

The third proviso to the use of the 1938 Act (that the person should not be interested in the proceedings) means that a social worker's statement of fact cannot normally be admitted since he will have been closely involved in instigating or defending proceedings and he is therefore an 'interested' person, see *R* v *Wood Green Crown Court ex parte P* (1983) 4 FLR 206. Finally, it should be noted that the only documentary statements admissible under s. 1 of the EA 1938 are ones of fact and not of opinion. The difference between the two can easily be blurred.

1.4.1 Approved certificates

Statute has prescribed that written evidence can be received by a juvenile court, without the need for the compiler of the evidence to attend, in the following situations. A certificate of a fully registered medical practitioner is admissible as evidence of a person's physical or mental condition, Children and Young Persons Act 1963, s. 26. This provision only allows a doctor to depose as to a child's medical condition and not as to the causes of that condition. Thus in some cases a certificate will be of little value, for example, proof of a broken arm does not normally reveal how it came about. Section 95 (2) (*c*) of the Education Act 1944 admits a certificate of the child's school attendance if it has been signed by the head teacher. This is a convenient way of establishing truancy, especially in care proceedings brought under s. 1 (2) (*e*) of the CYPA 1969.

1.4.2 Proof of convictions

It may be important to establish that a parent or other person, for example, a stepfather or the mother's boyfriend, has been convicted of a criminal offence, principally one involving violence. Under s. 11 of the CEA 1968, which applies to magistrates' courts, proof of a persons's conviction, whether he is a party to proceedings or not, is admissible provided that it is relevant to the current proceedings and that the conviction is a 'subsisting' one. The latter criterion is widely defined by s. 7 (2) (*c*) and (*d*) of the Rehabilitation of Offenders Act 1974 so that in relation to care proceedings convictions do not become 'spent'. Thus, if a person, when a teenager, was convicted of sexual assault on a child, the conviction will always be a 'subsisting' one for the purpose of proceedings under s. 1 (2) (*b*) or (*bb*) of the CYPA 1969. Similarly, a conviction for sexual assault on an adult is relevant (though it may be given less weight) when the offender is now alleged to have committed a sexual assault on a child. As for offences of violence against adults, these too are relevant and admissible in order to prove that the person has the capacity to be violent. They do not, of course, establish that he is liable to direct his violence towards a child. A 'conviction' includes a finding of guilt by a court-martial, CEA 1968, s. 11 (6), and it can be proved by, *inter alia*, a certified copy of the information, complaint, indictment or charge-sheet.

1.4.3. Documentary evidence at the 'reports' stage

The most common use of documentary evidence arises at the reports stage of care proceedings, that is, when the grounds of s. 1 of the CYPA 1969 have been established and the court is considering what order to make (see §4.5).

1.5 Corroboration

Judicial experience has led the law to provide that the testimony of certain individuals, though otherwise credible witnesses, needs to be supported, or corroborated, by independent evidence, or that a court should be wary of accepting the testimony without such support. Most development has taken place in the criminal law context with the following results. Prior to the Criminal Justice Act 1988 there were three pertinent rules. First, if a child gave evidence alleging, for example, maltreatment by his parents, the court had to warn itself as to the danger of accepting the child's evidence without corroboration. Secondly, if it was alleged that a sexual assault had been made against a child, a similar warning was needed since the victim of a sexual crime was involved and the law has always treated such an allegation with circumspection. Thirdly, if a child gave unsworn evidence, corroborative evidence had to be produced, CYPA 1933, s. 38. The Criminal Justice Act 1988 abolishes the first and third rules in relation to criminal proceedings. As for civil proceedings, it is doubtful whether the first two rules properly belong in the child-care context. If they do and the court's reasoning does not make it clear that the bench has administered to itself a corroboration warning, it is possible that an appeal could be lodged, or that a case could be stated for the High Court (compare the approach adopted in *Alli* v *Alli* [1965] 3 All ER 480, in relation to the old matrimonial offences). It is suggested that instead of adopting rigid rules the juvenile court should always address the issue of whether there is evidence to support the child's story and should be alert as to what is capable of amounting to supporting evidence. In this task the advice of lawyers in the case and, principally, of the justices' clerk is crucial. Failure to follow this suggested approach would usually warrant an appeal.

There are other situations where caution should prevail in the reception and handling of evidence even though no warning is required in law. In a case of alleged child abuse, for example, one spouse or cohabitee may be tempted to fabricate evidence in support of the other. Here the court is not bound to warn itself of the need for independent corroboration of the testimony for it is capable of amounting to corroborative evidence, but common sense dictates that the evidence may be of dubious quality.

1.6 Privileged or Protected Information

There is some information which is fully or partly prevented from disclosure between the parties and from production before the court, and some which a witness can choose not to disclose. There are four grounds for non-disclosure. The first seeks to protect the witness; the other three exist because of the confidential and sensitive nature of the information and the need to preserve that nature.

1.6.1 Privilege against self-incrimination

Before the juvenile court, a party or witness may refuse to answer any question or produce any document which would tend to expose him or his spouse to proceedings for a criminal offence, CEA 1968, s. 14. For example, a wife can refuse to answer questions which might expose her husband to prosecution for a crime of violence against their child. Since it is a privilege, it can be waived, wittingly or otherwise, by the witness. Its enforcement depends largely upon the vigilance of the lawyers present and of the court in intervening to prevent a line of questioning which would otherwise incriminate the witness. If the privilege is exercised, it is often likely to be counter-productive in the proceedings, since the court will proceed to weigh the evidence and will inevitably be swayed by the lack of explanation given by a witness in answer to a relevant question.

1.6.2 Legal privilege

Any information passing between a lawyer and his client for the purpose of giving legal advice is legally privileged provided that the professional relationship has been established between them. The privilege extends beyond lawyer/client communications so as to cover communications with a third party which have been made for the dominant purpose of preparing for actual or contemplated litigation. A report from a social worker commissioned by the child's parents is a simple example. In most cases the legal privilege will be waived since the party will want to rely upon the report at the hearing. But there will be a few cases where the report is adverse to the instructing party; for example, a social worker instructed by a parent may compile a report which is critical or equivocal about the parent's case. Only the parent can waive the privilege. If he chooses not to, the local authority and the child cannot see the report. Furthermore, even if the lawyer representing the parent wants the report to be disclosed to the court for the sake of the child's welfare, the decision is that of his client, the parent.

It will be noted that in order for a third party's evidence to attract legal privilege, its dominant purpose must be to prepare for litigation. Thus, routine medical, educational and social work reports on a child cannot qualify for legal privilege. However, protection for such information is not necessarily lost for it may fall within the next two categories.

1.6.3 Public interest immunity

The precise boundaries of public interest immunity in the child-care field are uncertain. The importance of determining them lies in the probability that the immunity cannot be waived (see §1.6.5). It is clear that the information requiring protection must be of a confidential nature, see *R* v *Bournemouth Justices ex parte Grey* [1987] 1 FLR 36; it is also clear that confidentiality alone is insufficient to attract the immunity. It must be allied to some other interest of public importance which justifies the maintenance of that confidentiality. Thus, in the leading case of *D* v *NSPCC* [1978] AC 171, information suggesting child abuse was passed to the NSPCC. The identity of the informant was held by the House of Lords to be immune from disclosure not solely because the information had been supplied in confidence, but because, if the informant's identity had been revealed, in the future others would be deterred from coming forward with information, and the NSPCC's important child-protection functions would be thwarted. For local authorities, protection of identities via public interest immunity will depend on the purpose for which the information is required. Thus, where allegations of ill-treatment of a child by its parents have been made to a local authority by neighbours and have been entered into the child's file, the authority may need to reveal the neighbours' identities to a juvenile court so that the case against the parents can be proved. It is clearly in the public interest that these witnesses be available to give evidence. If, on the other hand, parents or others are seeking the information from the local authority for non-child-care purposes (such as defamation proceedings), then public interest immunity will apply, on analogy with *D* v *NSPCC* (above).

Another, and more extensive, public interest which has been acknowledged is the need to ensure that agencies involved in child care can fulfil their statutory duties properly and without the constraining fear of being forced to divulge confidential information. Thus, if confidentiality will encourage candour and if this is essential to the child's wellbeing, the courts appear willing to extend protection to various types of information collected by a local authority about the child. *Re D (Infants)* [1970] 1 WLR 599 is an early example. There, case records compiled under the Boarding-Out of Children Regulations 1955 were held to be private, confidential and immune from discovery on grounds of public policy. The case was cited with approval in *D* v *NSPCC* (above). In *Gaskin* v *Liverpool CC* [1980] 1 WLR 1549 protection was further afforded to all the case notes and records of a boy who had been in care, and in *Re S and W (Minors)* (1982) 12 Fam. Law 151 it was extended to notes of a case conference. See also *Re M (Minors)* [1986] 1 FLR 46 and *R* v *Bournemouth Justices ex parte Grey*; *R* v *Bournemouth Justices ex parte Rodd* [1987] 1 FLR 36, where the question of immunity for the probation service and an adoption agency respectively was left undecided. It seems that this immunity can embrace notes, memoranda, interview records, a social worker's preliminary judgement on a client and other background information which contributes to a person's case record, and also to minutes or other records of case conferences and other reviews and discussion about the child and his family, *provided* that the information is so sensitive, or given in such sensitive circumstances, that the child-care services could not properly function if it were divulged. In cases of doubt, the court is entitled to see the documents to help it to determine whether the immunity applies to them.

1.6.4 Limitations to the immunity

The proviso stressed above is the crucial limitation to the width of public interest immunity. It was implicitly endorsed in *R v Greenwich Juvenile Court ex parte Greenwich LBC* (1977) 74 LGR 99, which rejected the practice whereby a local authority made a blanket assertion of privilege. It is not enough that the information concerns the child, nor even that it was given in confidence. Instead, documents must be considered individually to see if they qualify for protection because of the wider public interest outlined above. The proviso is also reflected in the DHSS Circular on Personal Social Service Records, LAC (83) 14. This stresses that not all information held about a client needs to be withheld and in fact it encourages local authorities to display a greater openness in revealing case records to clients and their representatives. There should, it directs, be a presumption that clients of social services departments (which include parents of children in care) should be allowed to see their records. In those areas where the local authority have implemented the spirit of the Circular, the practitioner's preparation of his case on behalf of parents can be greatly assisted. In those which are less forthcoming, he can at least point to the climate of openness which the Circular advocates. At the end of the day, however, it should be noted that public interest immunity covers a very wide range of documents and also that the practitioner is very dependent upon the local authority's discretion as to how much confidential information they are prepared to reveal.

1.6.5 Waiver of immunity

An important point to note about documents protected by public interest immunity is that the immunity probably cannot be waived by the party who holds them. The point has not been squarely decided, although the balance of opinion in *D v NSPCC* [1978] AC 171 supports the proposition. It means that there is much confidential information which a local authority cannot by law disclose even if they are amenable to disclosure.

1.6.6 Confidential and embarrassing information

There remains some information which, though not protected by public interest immunity or legal privilege, is still treated favourably because it is held in confidence. There are two situations to distinguish. First, the law of confidence can be used to prevent information from being passed to a third party. An example is afforded by the doctor and patient relationship. The law does not grant it a privilege from discovery. Furthermore, legal privilege will not protect information obtained by a doctor prior to the institution of legal proceedings since the doctor's purpose will have been the medical protection of his patient and not also the preparation for litigation, see §1.6.2. However, the doctor can rely on the confidentiality between him and his patient to defeat, for example, a request from parents that a child's medical records be handed over to their own doctor who has been instructed to appear in the proceedings. Confidentiality cannot, however, be used as a defence to a request for information made by a court. But in that event, the second situation may assist – provision may be made to prevent the undue disclosure of sensitive information. So, in the foregoing example, 'Courts have an inherent wish to respect this confidence' (Lord Wilberforce in *British Steel Corporation* v *Granada Television* [1981] AC 1096, at p. 1168) and will not compel a doctor to disclose confidential information unless it is necessary for the proper disposal of the proceedings. As for the reverse situation, where a doctor wishes to breach the confidentiality, it should be noted that both the British Medical Association and the medical defence societies have expressed the view that it is proper for a medical practitioner to initiate action to protect a child where abuse is suspected. The Council of the BMA has stated that, if a doctor has reason to believe that a child is being physically or sexually abused, not only is it permissible for the doctor to disclose information to a third party, but it is a duty of the doctor to do so.

Another protection for information can be found in the DHSS Circular LAC (83) 14 (above), which requires a local authority to obtain a third party's consent before information about him, or acquired from him, is disclosed. Furthermore, in care proceedings under the CYPA 1969 and in proceedings under the CCA 1980, it will be seen that the court has certain powers to hear evidence in the absence of the child and to exclude parents from the court whilst the child gives evidence (see §§4.4.3 and 4.4.4). The provisions are designed to avoid unnecessary embarrassment or trauma to the child and to encourage witnesses to give evidence.

1.7 Sexual Abuse

The type of evidence relied on in sexual abuse cases fits uneasily into the normal forensic framework of civil proceedings. Thus a local authority may prefer to bring the case in wardship, for here the High Court offers a more relaxed attitude to the rules of evidence than can a juvenile court. Also, a judge may better be able to assimilate and weigh conflicting opinion evidence from expert witnesses. However, before any court will make a finding that a child has been sexually abused it must be presented with a coherent and well-constructed argument that is supported by evidence. An allegation of sexual abuse can be especially difficult to substantiate because often the abuse (such as oral sex) gives rise to no physical symptoms. Other types produce symptoms which may also be consistent with non-abusing causes. Furthermore, expert witnesses may tend to disagree over the significance of physical signs or behavioural factors.

When sexual abuse is suspected the local authority may need to rely on the following types of evidence in order to prove their case: how the matter first came to light; medical findings (often equivocal or non-existent); an account of a disclosure interview with the child; a description of the child's behaviour; any problems observed at school; statements made by the alleged perpetrator; any relevant convictions of the alleged perpetrator; occasions where he or she had an opportunity sexually to abuse the child; a social assessment of the family. Much of this evidence will be hearsay. Where the child is exhibiting disturbed behaviour, the significance to be attributed to it will be informed by the opinion evidence of experts. Where reliance is placed on a disclosure interview with the child, interviewers need to be aware and appreciate that the manner of conducting the interview is crucial if its outcome is to be afforded any evidential weight.

Some guidance has been offered by the judiciary. The courts are unlikely to give weight to anything the child has said in response to leading questions. Other cues and prompts such as anatomically correct dolls must be used with great caution and the court will be alert to the child being put under pressure to allege sexual abuse, see *Re N (Minors)* [1987] 1 FLR 280. Judges are unhappy to accept an interviewer's account and interpretation of the interview with the child unless a transcript, carefully vetted for accuracy, and a videotaped recording are made available, *Re M (A Minor)* [1987] 1 FLR 293; *Re G (No. 2) (A Minor)* [1988] 1 FLR 314. Such transcripts and recordings permit another expert in the field to form a view, which is important where there is a dispute. Furthermore, the inherent risks in a court being willing to accept the unsupported statements and report of the interviewing expert were illustrated in *Re E* [1987] 1 FLR 269. Here the judge found that the interviewer's description of how the interview was conducted and what the child had said were not borne out by the videotaped recording.

It must be emphasized that there can be intervention and the child can be protected even though the court is not satisfied that the evidence points to any particular person as the perpetrator of the abuse. The standard to be satisfied is that of the balance of probabilities, *Re W (Minors)* [1987] 1 FLR 297. This enables a court to conclude that a child has been abused even though the available evidence falls far short of the standard of beyond reasonable doubt which would be needed for a conviction in criminal proceedings. It should be noted that in *Re G (No. 2) (A Minor)* (above) a distinction was drawn between the standard needed to establish that a child has been sexually abused, and that needed to name a parent as the abuser, where it was suggested that a higher degree of probability is required (but see §1.3.1).

1.8 Ethical Dilemmas

When a lawyer is approached by parents to represent their child in care proceedings under the CYPA 1969, he should be aware that it is the child and not the parents who is the party to the proceedings. Accordingly, the child is his client and, although he receives instructions from the parents, he is not bound to follow them. Where he forms the opinion that there is or may be a conflict between the interests of the child and those of his parents, he should inform the court. Steps can then be taken to ensure that child and parents are separately represented (see §4.1). In all the other child-care cases the parents but not the child are parties to the proceedings. However, the main concern of the court is to further the welfare of the child, Children and Young Persons Act 1933, s. 44, and this can sometimes pose a dilemma for the lawyer who represents the parents. For example, where they instruct him not to refer to evidence which is damaging to their chances of obtaining care of their child, what should he do?

His first and most obvious response is to urge the court to join the child as a party to the proceedings (see §§2.5.3 and 5.7.2). A guardian ad litem can then be appointed and he will normally instruct a solicitor for the child. The parent's solicitor may none the less need to resolve the dilemma of how far he should temper the presentation of his client's case in the child's interests. On the one hand, he is an officer of the court, with a duty not to mislead the court. On the other hand, his duty to his clients suggests that he is entitled to take full advantage of the adversarial framework to advance their interests. In a serious case, such as where he discovers on an occasion of legal and professional privilege that one of his clients has sexually assaulted the child, his remedy is to refuse to act for them. In a less serious case he will have to give careful consideration to balancing his duty to his clients against his duty to the court. There is no easy answer to this problem.

The local authority's lawyer can face a different but related dilemma. Many proceedings focus on the parents' fitness to care for their child, but social workers and others who are called as witnesses by the authority may still have to work with the family after the case has been decided. Consequently, a witness may be reluctant to exacerbate the situation by making specific allegations against the parents, or he may resort to speaking in euphemisms at the risk of being misunderstood and of concealing the gravity of the child's position. Furthermore, where an authority's witnesses give evidence in a relatively neutral manner the authority runs the risk of appearing less passionate and consequently less convincing than the parents. For example, the inquiry into the death of Wayne Brewer (1977) adverted to the fact that the authority's case against the revocation of a care order was put in 'a lower key altogether' than that advanced by the child's (in reality, the parents') solicitor. There is a fine line to be drawn between overstating and understating the arguments. In this dilemma it is suggested that the wellbeing of the child requires the authority's lawyer to err towards the former style.

1.9 Legal Aid

In addition to legal advice and assistance (the Green Form scheme), assistance by way of representation and legal aid are available for child-care and related proceedings in the following situations. In care proceedings under the CYPA 1969 the child is the person 'brought before a juvenile court' and thus qualifies for legal aid there and on appeal to the Crown Court, Legal Aid Act 1974 (LAA), s. 28 (3) and (6). Aid is granted if 'it appears to the court desirable to do so in the interests of justice', LAA 1974, s. 29 (1). As for the parent or guardian, he can only qualify if the court has made an order under s. 32A of the CYPA 1969 requiring that the child be separately represented, LAA 1974, s. 28 (6A) (and see §4.2). In both cases a grandparent is specifically included in the statutory scheme where he has been made a party to the proceedings under the CYPA 1969, s. 32C (and see §7.5.4). As for proceedings under Parts I and IA of the CCA 1980, assistance by way of representation is available. For those ineligible to qualify on financial grounds for this assistance, legal aid can be sought. It is available to those who have reasonable grounds for appearing at the proceedings, that is, the parent, and the child where the court has made him a party to the proceedings. Aid is not available to those who have no right, and who are not normally allowed, to be heard by the court, such as a grandparent who has no *locus standi*, LAA 1974, s. 7 (3). As for proceedings before the High Court in wardship or in pursuit of judicial review, legal aid is available in the normal way, LAA 1974, Sch. 1.

Child-care cases will frequently involve the use of expert witnesses. As far as legal aid is concerned, general authority to incur the costs of these witnesses and their reports is given by the Law Society and the maximum fee payable for such evidence is set down, Legal Aid (General) Regulations 1980, r. 61. It is open to the solicitor to apply for authority at a later stage to increase the fee payable or to acquire more reports, r. 62. As regards assistance by way of representation, a special request to the general committee must be made before expert witnesses can be instructed, Legal Advice and Assistance Regulations (No. 2) 1980, r. 17 (4). Particular difficulty can arise with regard to social workers instructed by parents. Their employment in child-related proceedings is out of favour with the courts (see §1.3.3) and it may be extremely difficult to justify their involvement for legal aid purposes.

With particular reference to wardship and chapter 6 of this book, it can be noted that the Official Solicitor has assisted the High Court in resolving many apparently intractable cases brought before it in wardship. But the increasing use of wardship and the consequential demands on the office of the Official Solicitor has resulted in a *Practice Direction* [1982] 1 WLR 118, under which a special reason for his involvement has to be established such as the complexity or controversial nature of the case. Apart from the delay in producing his report on the child for the court, there is the problem of costs. The court has an unfettered discretion in deciding costs, Supreme Court Act 1981, s. 51, and see *Re G (Minors) (Wardship: Costs)* (1982) 3 FLR 340. If a private litigant asks the Official Solicitor to intervene, the latter is fully entitled to ask for reimbursement of his costs. If a local authority seeks his assistance, negotiation between the two should settle the issue of costs and, if they cannot agree, the court will decide, see *Re G (Minors) (Wardship: Costs)* (above). When the court requests his intervention, the position is different. For, a judge should feel free to call upon the Official Solicitor 'without being constrained by the anxiety about the possible effect in relation to costs', *Re G (Minors) (Wardship: Costs)* (above). In this case the Official Solicitor is likely to bear his own costs out of the grant which is made available to his office out of central funds. It follows that the cheapest course for a litigant is to try to persuade the court to appoint the Official Solicitor of its own motion.

2 RECEPTION INTO CARE AND ASSUMPTION OF PARENTAL RIGHTS

2.1 Voluntary Care

It is generally accepted that a child's interests are usually best served by staying in his own family. The Child Care Act 1980 (CCA), which provides the framework for the reception of a child into care and for the subsequent duties and powers in relation to the child once he is in care, reflects this social policy. Section 1 places every local authority under a duty to make available such advice, guidance and assistance as may promote the welfare of children by diminishing the need to receive children into, or to keep them in, care. In addition to authorizing the provision of social work support, it empowers a local authority to provide services in kind or, in exceptional circumstances, in cash.

The way in which authorities comply with their duty under s. 1 varies. In some areas resources are severely limited, in others they are given priority. Quite apart from financial considerations, the effective use of s. 1 depends upon proper communication between the various departments of a local authority and often co-operation with other agencies. The types of assistance include day nursery care, home helps, housing, bed and breakfast accommodation and money to discharge rent, fuel and other debts. It is clear that a local authority should not fetter their discretion by adopting a rigid policy against granting help, for example, by refusing to house the intentionally homeless in all cases, *Attorney-General ex rel Tilley* v *Wandsworth LBC* (1981) 2 FLR 377. The authority can adopt a general policy of refusing, but they must consider each case, and must permit of exceptions from the general policy. But it should be noted that relief for an aggrieved parent, denied assistance under s. 1, is a remote possibility. An application in judicial review is the only remedy, and if successful this merely requires the local authority to consider the decision afresh and properly. For further consideration of judicial review, see §6.5.

More generally, however, s. 1 can often serve a useful role for practitioners. It can act as a yardstick for assessing a local authority's conduct in relation to a child, and as a supporting argument for reuniting parent and child.

2.1.1 Reception into care

Despite the provision of social work support and services, sometimes there is no alternative to reception of the child into care. Under s. 2 of the CCA 1980 a local authority have a duty to receive into care any child in their area appearing to be under the age of seventeen, if it appears to the authority:

(a) that he has neither parent nor guardian or has been and remains abandoned by his parents or guardian or is lost; or
(b) that his parents or guardian are, for the time being or permanently, prevented by reason of mental or bodily disease or infirmity or other incapacity or any other circumstances from providing for his proper accommodation, maintenance and upbringing; and
(c) in either case, that the intervention of the local authority under this section is necessary in the interests of the welfare of the child.

The reasons why parents are prepared voluntarily to give their child into local authority care are varied. Examples include homelessness, illness, a short-term emergency and difficulties with an adolescent. Their uniting feature is that the parents are prevented by circumstances from caring for their child, and have not made alternative private arrangements.

2.1.2 Rehabilitation

A local authority's primary duty towards a child in care is to safeguard and promote his welfare throughout his childhood, CCA 1980, s. 18. Where rehabilitation in the family is consistent with this duty, the local authority must endeavour to secure that the care of the child is taken over by his parents or guardian, or by a suitable relative or friend of the family, CCA 1980, s. 2 (3). Services and cash which are available to prevent reception into care, are also available to secure the return home of a child from care, CCA 1980, s. 1.

The entire focus of voluntary care is to secure the rehabilitation of a child with his family provided that this is consistent with his welfare.

2.1.3 No right to keep a child in voluntary care

A local authority have no right to keep a child in voluntary care against the wishes of the parent. Section 2 (3) of the CCA 1980 specifically provides that 'nothing in this section shall authorize a local authority to keep a child in their care under this section if any parent or guardian desires to take over the care of the child'. Theoretically, this provision is straightforward and is entirely consistent with a voluntary framework. Factually, the position may not be so straightforward. The local authority's primary duty is to promote the welfare of the child who is in their care. They may form the opinion that the parent is incapable of looking after the child properly, or that if the child goes home he will be ill-treated. Even when the parent is fit and able to care for the child, so much time may have elapsed since the child's reception into care that he may have formed very strong attachments to other adults who have been caring for him. For example, where a child has been in foster care, with little or no contact with his natural parents, it could prove a very distressing and traumatic experience for him to be taken, at short notice, from his foster home and sent back to his parents.

2.1.4 28 days' notice after six months in care

Section 13 (2) of the CCA 1980 contains a provision designed to facilitate the planned return of a child from care, and to give the local authority a 'breathing space' in which to consider whether removal from care would serve the child's best interests. Where the child has been in care for more than six months, the parent is required to give 28 days' notice in writing of his desire to have the child back again. The authority can, of course, return the child earlier. The parent should have been officially informed of this notice requirement at the time of the child's initial reception into care. If the parent removes the child from care during this 28-day period without first obtaining the local authority's consent, he commits a criminal offence, punishable with a maximum fine of £400, or three months in prison, or both.

Where the local authority decide that there are grounds to assume parental rights over the child, they have jurisdiction to pass a resolution under s. 3 of the Act during the 28-day period, see *Lewisham LBC* v *Lewisham Juvenile Court Justices* [1980] AC 273. This resolution vests the parental rights and duties in the local authority, and removes the right which the parent has under s. 2 (3) to take his child out of care.

2.1.5 Illegal removal by the parent

If the parent chooses to take his child from care without giving notice and to risk prosecution, the legal position is unclear. The local authority may wish immediately to recover physical possession of the child, but how can they best do so? The local authority have no right to obtain a warrant to recover a child who has been received into care under s. 2 of the CCA 1980. However, where the child has been the subject of a resolution passed under s. 3 of the Act, vesting parental rights and duties in the local authority, then a warrant to search for and remove the child can be issued under s. 15 (3). Can the local authority therefore pass a resolution under s. 3 of the Act and then seek a warrant to recover the child? The authority is faced with the difficulty that a parental rights resolution can only be passed in respect of a child who is 'in care under s. 2 of the Act'. It is not clear whether this includes a child who *should* still be in care, but who has been physically removed in breach of the requirement to give 28 days' notice.

In *Lewisham LBC* v *Lewisham Juvenile Court Justices* the House of Lords held that a child is in care until he is actually removed. This suggests that once a child has gone from care, the power to pass a resolution is lost. Only Lord Salmon gave direct consideration to whether a parental rights resolution can still be passed. He stated:

'. . . accordingly, if a parent, without having obtained the authority's consent or given the notice required by [s. 13 (2)], were to come to the authority *and take the child away* [our italics] or demand the immediate return of the child, this, in my view, would certainly not terminate the authority's care of the child under [s. 2] of the Act, nor its right to pass a parental resolution under [s. 3].' [1980] AC 273 at p. 291.

If Lord Salmon's view is correct, a local authority seeking recovery of a child removed in breach of the notice requirement could pass a resolution under s. 3, and then apply for a warrant under s. 15 (3). If his view is not followed, the authority's alternative course of action is to apply for a place of safety order under the Children and Young Persons Act 1969 (CYPA), s. 28 (1). However, the present tense drafting of many of the conditions in s. 1 (2) of that Act, which have to be satisfied, can mean that the authority have no evidence on which to base their application for a place of safety order. For the child has only just left care, he has been in care for at least the last six months, harm to him may be apprehended, but apprehended harm is not a ground for taking care proceedings under s. 1 (2) (*a*) of the CYPA 1969. Admittedly the child *is* in the hands of his parents, but until harm to him has occurred, there may be no ground for obtaining a place of safety order (see §§3.2 and 3.4.3). Consequently the local authority would have to contemplate the institution of wardship proceedings.

2.2 Power to Pass a Parental Rights Resolution

The assumption of parental rights and duties by resolution is a procedure which enables a local authority to take over the rights and duties of each parent individually in respect of his or her child. It is regarded by local authorities as a valuable procedure for safeguarding the position of a child who has no effective parent, and for protecting a child where the need for protection has arisen since the child came into care. Policy varies considerably. Some authorities use a resolution as a last resort, where the parents have lost all contact with the child, or where attempts have been made to rehabilitate the child over a long period, and these have failed. Other authorities pass a resolution soon after reception into care, and see it as a means of placing a child in long-term foster care, and even for adoption.

'Parental rights and duties' means in respect of a particular child all the rights and duties which by law the mother and father have in relation to a child and his property, Children Act 1975, s. 85 (1). However, ss. 3 (10) and 4 (3) of the CCA 1980 provide respectively that the assumption of parental rights does not give a local authority the right to consent to the child's adoption, or to cause the child to be brought up in a different religious creed. Where a court order has given legal custody to a third party, then, by virtue of s. 8 (2) of the CCA 1980, the third party enjoys the status of a parent or guardian; the third party's parental rights must be assumed, not the natural parent's rights, because it is the third party who has the right to remove the child from care. When implemented, the Family Law Reform Act 1987 (FLRA) will amend s. 8(2) so that it refers to *actual* custody, thus bringing the terminology into line with other legislation.

2.2.1 When is a child 'in care' under s. 2?

A parental rights resolution can only be passed in respect of a child already 'in care' under s. 2. The House of Lords held in *Lewisham LBC* v *Lewisham Juvenile Court Justices* [1980] AC 273 that a child does not cease to be in care when the parent notifies the local authority of his desire to take over the care of the child. It was their Lordships' unanimous view that care does not end until physical possession is taken over by the parent. But the question arises whether local authorities retain jurisdiction to pass a parental rights resolution in order to prevent immediate removal of the child, in a case where the child has been in care for less than six months.

The majority took the view that where the local authority wish to keep a child in care against the parent's wishes, they have no authority to do so under s. 2, but they will usually have a brief opportunity in which to pass a resolution under s. 3. Lord Salmon, however, took the view that:

> '. . . once a parent presents herself to the authority and demands the immediate return of her child who has been in the care of the authority for less than six months, the child ceases to be in the care of the authority under [s. 2] and accordingly the authority have no power to pass a parental resolution under [s. 3].' [1980] AC 273 at p. 291.

Lord Salmon emphasized this point by stating that the authority might well consider it to be their moral duty to keep the child in care long enough to have it made a ward of court, but this is 'all they could do to save the child'.

It is suggested that Lord Salmon's view is correct. The essence of care under s. 2 of the CCA 1980 is that it is voluntary care. If the provision in s. 2 (3) ('nothing in this section shall authorize a local authority to keep a child in their care under this section if any parent or guardian desires to take over the care of the child') is to retain any force, then care ends when the request is made and is accompanied by a willingness to take the child *at once*. Furthermore, if the voluntary principle underlying s. 2 were to lose its meaning, parents might then be encouraged to engage in unseemly forms of self-help, taking their child precipitately from care in order to prevent a resolution being passed. In this type of emergency wardship is available, and is the appropriate response where the child is at risk (see chapter 6).

For an example of a case where a local authority allegedly refused to allow a mother to see her children in s. 2 care, or to return them to her despite her requests to have them back, apparently without any legal authority, see *R* v *Local Commissioner for Administration ex parte Bradford MDC* [1979] QB 287.

2.2.2 Challenging the improper passing of a resolution

What courses of action are open to the parent if, having presented himself to the local authority within six months as ready and willing to take over the care of the child immediately, the authority refuse to release the child and instead pass a s. 3 resolution? The most useful remedy would be wardship proceedings but, as will be seen (§6.5), this remedy is no longer available to parents to challenge the actions of a local authority. The following options are available:

(1) The parent could object to the resolution, thereby forcing the local authority to lay a complaint in the juvenile court that the resolution should not lapse (see §2.5). He could then challenge the court's jurisdiction to hear and determine the complaint on the ground that the local authority had no power to pass the resolution.
(2) An order of certiorari could be sought to quash the resolution by applying for judicial review under RSC Ord. 53.
(3) A writ of habeas corpus could be issued.
(4) Civil proceedings for false imprisonment could be considered.

In some cases the threat of these proceedings will be sufficient to persuade the local authority to rescind the resolution. Where the local authority refuse, option (3) has the advantage over the others of speed. Application for it is made *ex parte* and the writ can be issued at once. Admittedly it has been suggested that habeas corpus proceedings are inappropriate in child cases (see *Re K (A Minor)* (1978) LSG 711) but in a case of the clearly unlawful holding of a child it could in fact be a very appropriate remedy, especially since the application for a writ must be made in the Family Division, RSC Ord. 54, r. 11, and since it has also been suggested that even in habeas corpus the High Court will have regard to the child's welfare (see *Re AB (An Infant)* [1954] 2 QB 385). The most sensible course would be for the court to direct that an originating summons be issued, in which case at least eight days will intervene before the hearing, RSC Ord. 54, r. 2. The local authority could in the meantime make their own *ex parte* application for wardship. Both actions could then be consolidated or heard by the same judge. For the consequential benefits of wardship, see chapter 6.

2.3 Grounds for a Parental Rights Resolution

The grounds for the assumption of parental rights are contained in s. 3 (1) (*a*) (*b*) (*c*) and (*d*) of the CCA 1980.

2.3.1 Paragraph (a)

That his parents are dead and he has no guardian or custodian. This paragraph enables a local authority to assume parental rights over an orphan. If the child is an illegitimate child, then only his mother is recognized in law as his parent. His natural father may fall within the formal definition of 'guardian', which means a person who has been appointed by deed or will or by a court, CCA 1980, s. 87 (1), or he may wish to apply for guardianship under s. 5 (1) of the Guardianship of Minors Act 1971 (GMA) (see §7.4). Alternatively, when the FLRA 1987 is implemented, the father will qualify as a 'parent' if he has already obtained a parental rights order under s. 4 of that Act.

Because s. 8 (2) of the CCA 1980 provides that a person with custody under a court order is to be treated as the child's parent or guardian for the purposes of ss. 1–7 of the CCA 1980, this appears to have the consequence that, in the case of married or divorced parents, if the custodial parent dies, the child, as a matter of law, has no parent or guardian. It could be argued to the contrary that on the custodial parent's death, the court order lapses and custody automatically reverts to the surviving parent. But that interpretation is contrary to the express wording of s. 8 (2) and, more importantly, could have the unfortunate effect of enabling a parent, who has shown no or little interest in the child's welfare, to thwart an authority's action under para. (*a*). A person with custody does not mean a person who has simply been looking after the child. It means a person who has been given legal custody of the child by a court order (or actual custody when the FLRA 1987 is implemented, see above).

2.3.2 Paragraph (b)

Section 3 (10) of the CCA 1980 provides that for the purposes of para. (*b*), 'parent' includes a guardian or custodian. This paragraph, divides into five sub-paragraphs and covers the parent who has abandoned his child; or who is incapable of caring for him; or who is unfit to care for him:

(1) *That a parent has abandoned the child.* Abandoned is used in the sense of deserting the child and leaving him to his fate. It was held in *Wheatley* v *London Borough of Waltham Forest* [1979] 2 WLR 543 that the parent's conduct must be culpable and of a type which would render him liable to prosecution. In Wheatley's case the mother left her child in the care of his grandmother and disappeared. It was found by the Divisional Court that she had been feckless and irresponsible, but that she did not thereby abandon her child. Abandonment would

clearly cover the situation where a mother leaves her newborn baby wrapped in a sheet on a park bench. Whether it covers a mother who leaves her child in the offices of her local social services department while she goes away for the weekend with her boyfriend is debatable. It must be the parent who abandons the child; if it is the child's grandmother, for example, who leaves the child to his fate, the mother's parental rights cannot be assumed on this ground, *Crosby (A Minor)* v *Northumberland CC* (1982) 12 Fam. Law 92.

Sometimes the situation arises where the parent gradually loses contact with the child and the local authority, and it is not clear whether or not the parent intends to resume contact again. Section 3 (8) offers assistance by providing that a parent shall be deemed to have abandoned his child if the parent's whereabouts have remained unknown for twelve months after the child came into care.

The child must still be abandoned at the time when the resolution is made, so if the parent has resumed contact with the child before the resolution is passed he is no longer abandoned, see *Wheatley* v *London Borough of Waltham Forest* (above) where a mother visited her child regularly over several months preceding the resolution.

(2) *That a parent suffers from some permanent disability rendering him incapable of caring for the child.* The disability may be either physical or mental. It must be permanent and must render the parent incapable of caring. The age of the child will be a relevant consideration; a disabled parent may be incapable of looking after a baby or toddler properly, but able to provide adequate care for an older child. It is also pertinent to consider what types of assistance have been provided, under s. 1 of the CCA 1980, to enable the parents to look after their own child and to avoid reception into care.

(3) *That a parent while not falling within subpara. (2) suffers from a mental disorder (within the meaning of the Mental Health Act 1983), which renders him unfit to have the care of the child.* 'Mental disorder' is defined by s. 1 (2) of the Mental Health Act 1983 as meaning 'mental illness, arrested or incomplete development of mind, psychopathic disorder and any other disorder or disability of mind'. The flexibility and imprecision of this definition are self-evident. There is no requirement in the case of mental illness that the illness should be permanent. It could be intermittent, or it could be of a temporary nature only. The crucial question is whether it renders the parent unfit to have the care of the child. Fitness to care is a more evaluable

notion than capacity to care, and expert evidence from a psychiatrist is generally desirable.

(4)   *That a parent is of such habits or mode of life as to be unfit to have the care of the child.* The behaviour complained of must be habitual. The words 'habits or mode of life' are broad and are capable of covering a variety of situations such as drug addiction, alcoholism, persistent criminality, prostitution and vagrancy. The parent's fitness to care is tested against current standards of conduct and morality. These standards vary, and it is alleged that they enable social workers to impose their own subjective values on families who deviate from the norm.

(5)   *That a parent has so consistently failed without reasonable cause to discharge the obligations of a parent as to be unfit to have the care of the child.* It has been stressed in the High Court that to divest a parent of parental rights and duties is a very serious decision, and to justify it under this ground the conduct of the parent must be highly culpable, *Wheatley* v *London Borough of Waltham Forest* (above); *O'Dare Ai* v *South Glamorgan CC* (1982) 3 FLR 1. The obligations of a parent include not only the legal duty to maintain the child but also the moral duty to show the child affection, care and interest, *Re P (Infants)* [1962] 1 WLR 1296.

Three matters must be proved. First, that the failure has been consistent. This is not the same as persistent. It need not have continued over a substantial length of time, but it must have been consistently adhered to over the length of time of which complaint is made, *W* v *Sunderland BC* (1981) 2 FLR 153; *M* v *Wigan MBC* (1980) 1 FLR 45. The question to ask is 'is there a pattern in the behaviour?' Failure to visit a child in care may be sufficient, but there must be a callousness and self-indulgent indifference on the part of the parent, *M* v *Wigan MBC* (above); *O'Dare Ai* v *South Glamorgan CC* (above).

Secondly, it must be proved that the parent's failure has been without reasonable cause. If there is a genuine reason for the failure, there is a reasonable cause. If, for example, a local authority limit visits to the child to three hours once a week (as in *Wheatley* v *London Borough of Waltham Forest* (above)), they cannot then rely on failure to visit for the assumption of parental rights. If the parent does not have the means to visit the child, or is unable to do so because he is in hospital, the ground cannot be proved. If the parent is in prison the position is problematic. If he commits a crime which results in a lengthy term of imprisonment, it is difficult to see how he thereby consistently fails to discharge his parental obligations, even allowing for a generous interpretation of 'consistent'. For example, a parent could be in prison for a first offence, such as serious fraud. He may be very concerned about his child, even though he is not presently able to discharge his obligations. On the other hand, where a parent has been regularly convicted and imprisoned, his behaviour is consistent, and it is arguable that he has brought his predicament on himself and therefore has been culpable.

A parent who is psychologically or emotionally inadequate may not be culpable. The authorities differ on whether the test to be applied is objective or subjective. In *O'Dare Ai* v *South Glamorgan CC* (above) the Divisional Court held that the local authority must prove blameworthy conduct involving a subjective departure by the parent from a proper standard of conduct which can be regarded as morally reprehensible. However, in *M* v *Wigan MBC* (above) the Divisional court held that an objective standard is appropriate, that is, the court must look to see whether the conduct was reasonable or unreasonable according to what a reasonable parent would have done in all the circumstances. It is suggested that this latter approach is to be preferred. It more naturally accords with the wording of s. 1 (*b*) (v), and with the spirit of the legislation, and it is in line with the similarly worded Scottish legislation, see *Central Regional Council* v *B* (1985) SLT 413.

The third matter to be proved is that the parent is unfit to care for the child. Consistent rejection of the children by their parents led to this condition being satisfied in *M* v *Wigan MBC* (above). But where there is regular contact between parent and child, and where failure to visit or take the child out of care has been caused partly through the parent's fault, but not in a truly culpable sense, the high standard required for proof of unfitness to care is not satisfied, *W* v *Sunderland BC* (above).

The child's long-term welfare and the parent's culpability may turn on quite different considerations (for a particularly acute example of this see *W* v *Nottinghamshire CC* (1982) 3 FLR 33). Research by M. Adcock, R. White and O. Rowlands (published as *The Administrative Parent*) suggests that local authorities focus more closely on the needs and welfare of the child and how the child is being affected by the parent's behaviour, rather than on the culpability of the parent. This may mean that facts accepted by a local authority as justifying a resolution under this paragraph, would not be found adequate if challenged in a court, particularly the High Court. The few reported cases cited above also suggest that a juvenile court is more inclined to be influenced by considerations of the child's welfare, because in each case the juvenile court ordered that the resolution should not lapse. This may be because the juvenile court, unlike the High Court, cannot point one of the parties in the direction of wardship if it is uneasy about the child's welfare.

Where the parent has successfully appealed to the High Court, the local authority have sometimes resorted to wardship, *O'Dare Ai* v *South Glamorgan CC* (above); *Crosby* v *Northumberland CC* (above). The role of wardship can be vital in a case where an indifferent or feckless parent (for example the mother in *Wheatley*) has only partially fulfilled her obligations to the child, particularly those of showing affection, care and interest in the child. If that parent later seeks to reassert her parental rights, the child may in the meanwhile have settled contentedly with foster-parents with whom he has a secure home; adoption may even be planned (as in *W* v *Sunderland BC* (above)). Wardship allows the court to give first and paramount consideration to the child's welfare when deciding the child's future (see §6.3.2).

2.3.3 Paragraph (c)

That a resolution under para. (b) of this subsection is in force in relation to one parent of the child who is, or is likely to become, a member of the household comprising the child and his other parent. A local authority must have grounds for assuming each parent's parental rights individually. This paragraph can be relied on to prevent the parent who retains his parental rights from removing the child from care and taking it to live with the parent whose rights have already been assumed under para. (*b*).

2.3.4 Paragraph (d)

That throughout the three years preceding the passing of the resolution the child has been in the care of a local authority under s. 2 of this Act, or partly in the care of a local authority and partly in the care of a voluntary organization. Here there is no need to prove culpability or unfitness to care on the part of the parent. Consequently, it may be more acceptable to parents than the other grounds which highlight parental weaknesses and may thus damage a parent's self-respect. Where a child has been in care for years he may often have no real relationship with his natural parents. His deepest feelings, loyalties and attachments are to others, for example, foster-parents. Any attempt to remove the child from his present home could prove traumatic and damaging (for example, see *W* v *Nottinghamshire CC* (1982) 3 FLR 33). The lapse of three years enables local authorities to assume parental rights in order to protect the child from removal from care, where this is believed to be against his best interests. One purpose of this provision is to enable plans to be made for a child who might otherwise drift into long-term care. Sometimes it is used as a preliminary to the institution of an adoption or custodianship application by long-term foster-parents. It secures the foster-parents' position, and prevents the abrupt removal of the child should the parents oppose the adoption or custodianship plan.

2.4 Procedures

2.4.1 The Social Services Committee meeting

The decision to assume parental rights is made by members of the Social Services Committee of the local authority, usually by a specialist sub-committee. A senior officer of the Social Services Department puts a report before the elected members, and gives the Department's reasons for believing that it is necessary to assume the parent's rights. The Committee should also be told about the Department's future plans for the child.

2.4.2 The role of the parents

Local arrangements vary on whether parents are given the opportunity to be heard by members of the committee before their parental rights are assumed. Some local authorities permit the parent to attend all or part of the meeting, to bring a friend, and to address the committee members. Others merely permit the parents to make their views known in writing. Others arrange for the parents to meet some members of the committee (including usually the chairman) before the meeting is held.

It has been stated in a circular issued by the DHSS to local authorities that, whatever local procedures are agreed, parents should have prior notice of the content of the report prepared by the Social Services Department. Either they should receive a copy of the report, or they should have a written statement of the facts which are to be put before the members of the committee (LAC (84) 5 Parental Rights Resolutions, paras. 19 and 29).

2.4.3 The role of the solicitor

At this stage the parent may be advised to approach a solicitor to seek advice on how to prepare a written statement for the committee. The fact that the local authority have earlier obtained the parent's consent to the proposed resolution does not bind the parent, or prevent him from changing his mind. In providing assistance, the solicitor should bear in mind that the facts relied on by the local authority must support one of the statutory grounds for a resolution. In an appropriate case he may wish to challenge the accuracy of some of the facts alleged; or he may wish to challenge the appropriateness of a s. 3 resolution to the circumstances. He may also seek to ascertain, on behalf of his client, what plans the local authority have for the future of the child once they have assumed parental rights over him.

Some local authorities may be willing to allow the solicitor to attend the meeting at which the proposal for a resolution will be considered. However, local authorities have been advised that 'in devising procedures for such meetings, every effort should be made to achieve informality as far as possible and particularly to avoid the appearance of judicial function. The aim should be to avoid cross-questioning of each other by parents or social workers' (LAC (84) 5, para. 26).

It seems, therefore, that at this stage the solicitor has only a limited part to play in assisting the parent in opposing a parental rights resolution. He may be able to persuade a local authority, which grants only restricted rights of audience to the parent (or occasionally no such rights at all) to operate a more generous system in the light of the guidance issued by the DHSS. However, it should be noted that the conduct of the meeting of the Social Services Committee lies within the discretion of the local authority; the only right conferred on the parent by statute is to object to the resolution after it has been passed.

2.4.4 Objecting to a s. 3 resolution

A parent must be given notice of a s. 3 resolution immediately after it has been passed. The notice should be informative and helpful. It should clearly set out the statutory grounds for the resolution (*Re L (AC) (An Infant)* [1971] 3 All ER 743 is an illustration of how this should *not* be done), and it should contain a simple tear-off portion which can be returned if the parent objects (LAC (84) 5, para. 31).

Where the parent objects, he must serve a counter-notice in writing on the local authority within one month (hence the need for the parent to be provided with a simple form on which to do so). The resolution will lapse on the expiry of fourteen days from the service of the counter-notice unless, within that period, the authority make a complaint to the juvenile court. In that event the resolution does not lapse until the matter is determined by the court, CCA 1980, s. 3 (2) (3) (4) and (5).

2.5 The Juvenile Court Hearing

2.5.1 What must be proved?

The local authority is the complainant in the juvenile court and has the burden of proof. It must therefore be stressed that care should be taken at all stages to prepare the case thoroughly and to obtain full evidence which will survive judicial scrutiny. The court may order that the resolution shall not lapse only if it is satisfied of each of the following conditions:

(1) that the grounds on which the local authority purported to pass the resolution were made out when the resolution was passed;
(2) that at the time of the hearing there continue to be grounds on which a resolution could be founded; and
(3) that it is in the interests of the child that the resolution should not lapse (CCA 1980, s. 3 (6)).

It is not necessary for the local authority to prove that the ground on which the resolution was originally passed still exists on the day of the hearing. Provided that there continues to be a ground on which a resolution could now be founded, albeit a different one, the court can order the resolution to remain in force. An example is *W* v *Nottinghamshire CC* (1982) 3 FLR 33. There the local authority passed a resolution under s. 3 (1) (*b*) (v). When the matter came before the court in the first instance, it was agreed between the parties that the case should be adjourned for a year to enable contact to be built up between mother and child. During that period the mother co-operated fully with the social workers, but the access arrangements caused so much distress to the child that after about three months they were stopped by the local authority. At the date of the resumed hearing the child had been in care for more than three years. It was held in the Court of Appeal that what the court must consider at the date of the hearing is whether the local authority could now lawfully pass a s. 3 resolution, but not necessarily a resolution founded on the same ground as that relied on for the original assumption of parental rights. The Scottish provisions are to similar effect, see *Central Regional Council* v *B* (1985) SLT 413.

In contrast, the court's finding that the parent is not now a fit and proper person to have custody of the child is not sufficient if, originally, there was no ground for passing the resolution, *Crosby (A Minor)* v *Northumberland CC* (1982) 12 Fam. Law 92. Consequently, even if at the date of the hearing a ground exists and care is in the child's interests, the resolution must lapse where a ground did not exist at the earlier stage. In such a case, if the child returns to the parent he should be placed on the 'at risk' register, and care proceedings may soon follow. Furthermore, wardship should always be considered by an authority in a case of this kind.

2.5.2 Challenging a s. 3 resolution

When challenging the assumption of parental rights the parent's lawyer should test the evidence in two main respects. He should test first whether there were and still are grounds for a resolution, and secondly he should test the local authority's assertion that the assumption of parental rights is in the interests of the child. The position may best be clarified if the lawyer directs his questioning and cross-examination of witnesses to earlier social work approaches to the case, to the priority given to attempts to rehabilitate the child with his family, and to the local authority's future plans for the child. To this end it may be useful for the lawyer to include in his questions some or all of the following matters.

What efforts have been made by social workers to make available advice, guidance and assistance to the parent? Have the local authority complied with their duty under s. 1 of the CCA 1980 to give assistance in kind, or, in exceptional circumstances, in cash where this will diminish the need to receive children into or keep them in care? For example, has assistance been offered in the form of home helps, day care, nursery care, peripatetic house-parents, provision of housing (even if the family has become intentionally homeless), or cash to pay debts such as rent arrears or fuel bills? If this type of assistance has not been forthcoming, or appears to have been inadequate, the lawyer could highlight the link between the local authority's duties under s. 1 and the grounds for assumption of parental rights under s. 3. The loss of a child is a grave matter, and where it is alleged that a parent is incapable of caring or is unfit to care, the lawyer should explore how far this is due to the fault of the parent and how far it is due to poverty and material deprivation, much of which is beyond the parent's control.

The lawyer should attempt to explore whether, if help under s. 1 were to be offered, the parent would be able to resume caring for his child. Where the parent's desire or willingness to be involved in his child's future upbringing is being doubted by a social worker, it is often pertinent to ask the social worker how much social work contact has been maintained with the parent since the child was received into care. If the parent has visited the child only sporadically, is this because it was difficult, geographically and financially, for visits to be made? Was the parent consulted about the child's placement? What efforts have been made to maintain close contact between parent and child? What attempts have been made to rehabilitate the child with his family?

Some local authorities tend to make an early decision to sever all links between the child and his family in order to impose a 'clean break', and to provide the child with a substitute long-term family, often with a view to adoption. The lawyer could seek to discover what is motivating the local authority in their decision to assume parental rights. Is it because the natural parent is unfit or unable to care, or is it because a substitute home appears to offer better long-term prospects for the child? Do the authority intend to deny the parent access to his child? Do they intend to take steps to facilitate the child's adoption? If this is the position, the lawyer could challenge whether severance of the parental link with the child through the assumption of parental rights is in the child's best long-term interests.

2.5.3 Protecting the child's interests

In contrast to care proceedings under the CYPA 1969, the child is not automatically a party to proceedings under s. 3 (6) of the CCA 1980. However, in any case where the court considers it necessary that he should be made a party in order to safeguard his interests, it can make an order that he should be joined and appoint a guardian ad litem, CCA 1980, s. 7 (1). Rule 31 (1) of the CYP Rules 1988 provides that a guardian ad litem must be appointed unless the court is satisfied that to do so is not necessary in order to safeguard the interests of the child. It is suggested that the solicitors for both parties, but especially the local authority's solicitor, should be alert to the possibility of the court concentrating its attention on the parents' qualities, and of the child's interests becoming submerged. It may often be appropriate for either or both of them to urge the court to join the child as a party and to appoint a guardian ad litem.

The guardian ad litem decides whether to instruct a solicitor for the child. The solicitor takes his instructions from the guardian ad litem, unless the child wishes to give his own instructions which conflict with those of the guardian ad litem; where this happens the solicitor is instructed by the child, r. 31 (6) (*d*). Clearly, the solicitor should interview the child before the hearing to discover his views and to see whether he needs to make his own assessment of the case on behalf of the child. This is particularly apposite where the guardian ad litem supports the assumption of parental rights, but where the child wishes to live with his parents, or vice versa.

2.6 Rescission of a Parental Rights Resolution

A s. 3 resolution remains in force until the child attains the age of
eighteen. It ceases to have effect if the child is adopted, or a guardian
of the child is appointed under s. 5 of the Guardianship of Minors
Act 1971 (GMA) (see §7.4). The local authority can at any time
rescind the resolution where this appears to be for the child's benefit,
CCA 1980, s. 5 (1) (2) and (3). In reaching a decision the authority
must give first consideration to the need to safeguard and promote
the welfare of the child throughout his childhood; and shall so far as
practicable ascertain the wishes and feelings of the child regarding
the decision and give due consideration to them, having regard to
his age and understanding, CCA 1980, s. 18 (1). This should normally
prevent the rescission of a parental rights resolution in a case where
the child wishes to remain in care.

2.6.1. Termination by a juvenile court

An application can be made to a juvenile court, at any time, for the
resolution to be rescinded. Section 5 (4) of the CCA 1980 provides
that on a complaint being made:

(a) in the case of a resolution passed by virtue of s. 3 (1) (*a*) of
    this Act, by a person claiming to be a parent, guardian or
    custodian of the child;
(b) in the case of a resolution passed by virtue of s. 3 (1) (*b*), (*c*)
    or (*d*) of this Act, by the person who, but for the resolution,
    would have the parental rights and duties in relation to the
    child,
    a juvenile court having jurisdiction where the complainant resides,
    if satisfied that there was no ground for the making of the resolution
    or that the resolution should in the interests of the child be
    determined, may by order determine the resolution, and the
    resolution shall thereupon cease to have effect.

The child can be joined as a party and have his interests protected
through the appointment of a guardian ad litem and legal representation, in the manner described above (§2.5.3).

It should be noted that under s. 5 (4), the parent has the burden
of proof. Furthermore, where he seeks to prove that there was no
ground for the making of the resolution he must lay his complaint
within six months of the resolution being passed, Magistrates' Courts
Act 1980, s. 127. Even where the parent is able to establish the truth
of this allegation the court is not bound to determine the resolution;

the Act says it may do so, not that it shall, and see *K* v *Devon CC* (1987) 17 Fam. Law 348. This is in sharp contrast to the detailed criteria which must be satisfied before the court can order that the resolution shall not lapse under s. 3 (6) of the CCA 1980; and see *Re L(AC) (An Infant)* [1971] 3 All ER 743.

The parent must also show that it is in the child's interests that the resolution be determined. The Act does not state that the child's interests are the court's first and paramount consideration, nor does it provide guidance on how much weight should be given to the parent's claim to look after his own child. Section 5 (4) specifies the sole criterion of the child's interests. However, since parental disability or unfitness will have necessitated the resolution, it is understandable that the court will wish to look at the current position of the parents. On the other hand, the court would be wrong to confine itself to considering parental capacity and fitness to care. The interests of the child, especially after a lengthy period in care, will frequently raise other options for the court to consider. For example, the child may have been placed with foster-parents with a view to adoption. In such a case the local authority's lawyer (and the child's lawyer where one has been appointed) should stress that the child's interests, and not the fitness of the parents, are the statutory criterion.

2.7 Appeals

Any party to proceedings brought under ss. 3 (6) or 5 (4) of the CCA 1980 (including the child if he has been made a party) can appeal as of right to the Family Division of the High Court, CCA 1980, s. 6. An appeal must be launched by notice of motion within six weeks, and three copies of various documents (including the justices' clerk's notes and the justices' reasons for the decision) must be lodged at the principal registry of the Family Division, RSC Ord. 90, r. 16. The appeal is by 'way of rehearing', RSC Ord. 90, r. 3 (1) and consequently the child can be made a party to the appeal and a guardian ad litem can be appointed, CCA 1980, s. 7. The High Court can consider points of law or facts or both, and can receive fresh evidence on questions of fact. However, it is not bound to allow an appeal 'on the ground merely of misdirection or improper reception or rejection of evidence unless, in the opinion of the court, substantial wrong or miscarriage of justice has been thereby occasioned', RSC Ord. 90, r. 16 (6).

It should be noted that some of the cases taken on appeal from a decision made under s. 3 (6) of the CCA 1980 (for example, *Wheatley* v *London Borough of Waltham Forest* [1979] 2 WLR 543; *O'Dare*

Ai v *South Glamorgan CC* (1982) 3 FLR 1; *Crosby (A Minor)* v *Northumberland CC* (1982) 12 Fam. Law 92) have ultimately been resolved by the High Court exercising its wardship jurisdiction. Where the local authority are the appellant they could be well advised to make the child a ward. This approach enables the High Court to give first and paramount consideration to the welfare of the child, and to make an order more properly suited to the child's care and upbringing than the 1980 Act's narrow range of orders, which merely require the resolution to be upheld or terminated (see chapter 6).

3 GROUNDS FOR CARE PROCEEDINGS

3.1 Foundation of Care Proceedings

The foundation of care proceedings is that one or more of seven specified conditions applies to a child or young person, and that he is in need of care or control which he is unlikely to receive unless the court makes an order, Children and Young Persons Act 1969 (CYPA), s. 1 (2). A child or young person must be under seventeen, but an order cannot be made where he is sixteen and where he is or has been married, CYPA 1969, s. 1 (5) (c). Henceforth 'child' is used to include young person. Care proceedings can be taken in respect of three types of children who can be loosely categorized as: the neglected and ill-treated, the troublesome and the truant, and the juvenile offender. In practice, care proceedings are rarely taken in respect of juvenile offenders. Instead such children are cautioned or prosecuted under the normal criminal process. This means that applications under s. 1 (2) of the CYPA 1969 are made when the child is coming to harm or is threatened with harm (physical, mental or moral), where he is beyond control, or where he is not going to school.

Any local authority, constable, or authorized person (at present only the NSPCC), who reasonably believe that there are grounds for making an order, may bring a child before the court. In almost all cases the applicant is the local authority.

Often the decision to institute care proceedings is made at a case conference, where individuals and representatives of various agencies meet to decide what action should be taken in respect of a child believed to be at risk. At this stage it is often advisable for a lawyer to be present. He can guide the participants on the types of evidence necessary to satisfy the court that there is ground for intervention. Where an application in care proceedings is ill-prepared it may be dismissed; or the court may make a supervision order rather than the care order sought by the local authority. This can be disastrous for the child. An application which fails may expose the child to even

41

greater risk because the parent may no longer trust his doctor, health visitor, social worker or anyone else in a position to keep a watchful eye on the child. Accordingly it must be emphasized that the application should be well prepared from the outset.

3.2 Place of Safety Orders

Place of safety orders are often obtained as a preliminary to care proceedings to secure the immediate removal of a child from his home. Any person may apply under s. 28 (1) of the CYPA 1969 for authority to detain a child and take him to a place of safety. It is suggested, however, that an application should usually be made only in an emergency. The applicant must satisfy a single justice (not necessarily trained in juvenile matters) that he has reasonable cause to believe that any of the conditions set out in s. 1 (2) (*a*)–(*e*) of the CYPA 1969 is satisfied, or that the court would find condition (*b*) satisfied, or that the child is about to leave the United Kingdom as an entertainer without a licence. The applicant is in a strong position since it will take a brave justice to refuse to make an order. The justice can order the child to be detained in a place of safety (defined, broadly, as a community home provided by a local authority or a controlled community home, any police station, hospital, surgery or any other suitable place, the occupier of which is willing temporarily to receive a child, Children and Young Persons Act 1933 (CYPA), s.107 (1) as amended) for a maximum period of 28 days; often a shorter period is granted.

A place of safety order does not give the applicant the right to enter premises and remove the child without the householder's consent. Where entry is refused or is likely to be refused, a warrant can be obtained under s. 40 of the CYPA 1933. It can be sought at the same time as the place of safety hearing. The criteria set out in that section and s. 15 of the Police and Criminal Evidence Act 1984 (PACE) must be satisfied and the warrant must be executed in accordance with s. 16 of the latter Act. Certain actions are deemed to constitute reasonable suspicion for the issue of a warrant. In essence they consist of refusing to allow a child to be visited or examined, or to allow certain premises to be inspected (CYPA 1969, s. 14A; Adoption Act 1976, s. 37 (1); CCA 1980, s. 75 (3); Foster Children Act 1980, s. 13 (2); Children's Homes Act 1982, s. 9 (5)). Where speed is essential to protect a child and a warrant will take too long to obtain, s. 17 (1) (*e*) of PACE 1984 empowers a constable to enter premises in order to save life or limb. This is a useful power because the constable is absolved from the need to show that he had reasonable grounds for believing that the child was on the premises, PACE 1984, s. 17 (2) (*a*). If necessary, he can use reasonable force to enter the premises, PACE 1984, s. 117.

3.2.1 Emergency powers of a constable

A further emergency power is open to any constable who has reasonable cause to believe that any condition in s. 1 (2) (*a*)–(*d*) is satisfied or that s. 1 (2) (*b*) would be satisfied or that a vagrant is unlawfully taking a juvenile from place to place. He can detain the child for up to eight days on the authority of a senior officer, CYPA 1969, s. 28 (4).

The power does not entitle entry on to premises. For that, consent of the occupier, a warrant under s. 40 of the CYPA 1933 or entry under s. 17 (1) (*e*) of PACE 1984 will be needed. Unlike a place of safety order, the child or, more usually, his parent or guardian can challenge the detention before a magistrate, CYPA 1969, s. 28 (5). The police are entitled to be notified of the application, to be heard and to give evidence, *R* v *Bristol Justices ex parte Broome* [1987] 2 FLR 76. The subsection goes on to provide that release *shall* be ordered unless the child's interests dictate to the contrary – a loose test which will favour the detainer. This power of detention is essential for those urgent cases where a constable or other person, for example, a neighbour, stumbles upon a suspected case of child abuse or where there is insufficient time to alert and consult the local authority's social services department.

3.2.2 The parents' position

The parents must be told about the child's detention and the reason for it as soon as is practicable, CYPA 1969, s. 28 (3), but at this stage they have no rights. They are not entitled to be heard when the application for a place of safety order is made, and they cannot appeal against it. If denied access to their child during the subsistence of the order, they have no right to appeal the decision to a court. Furthermore, in *Nottinghamshire CC* v *Q* (1982) 3 FLR 305 it was held that an application by a parent under s. 28 (6) of the CYPA 1969 for an interim order, with the express purpose of obtaining the release of the child from care, was an improper application and an abuse of the process of the court. Similarly, an attempt through wardship to secure the child's release will fail, *Re E (Minors) (Wardship: Jurisdiction)* (1983) 4 FLR 668. The maximum period for which a place of safety order can be granted is 28 days. Concern that this is unduly long for the parents means that in some areas magistrates will normally grant an order for a shorter period, such as eight days. Where the local authority wish to detain the child for longer they must swiftly make an application to a juvenile court for an interim order under s. 28 (6) of the CYPA 1969. The parent has a right to be heard in these proceedings, *H* v *London Borough of Southwark* (1982) 12 Fam. Law 211.

3.2.3 Medical examination of the child

When a child has been removed from home under a place of safety order it may be thought essential or desirable that he is medically examined and treated. This can give rise to difficulties for, while the effect of the order is to transfer responsibility for the child to the applicant and the right to decide where he will live, it does not transfer all other parental rights. The right to consent to medical examination and treatment remains vested in the parent(s). Where consent is not forthcoming the legal position is somewhat opaque. It is stated in DHSS Circular (88) 2 (*Medical Examination of a Child Subject to a Place of Safety Order*) that where a doctor has reasonable cause to believe that medical treatment may be needed he may examine the child for the purpose of assessment for such treatment. If it transpires that treatment is urgently required, only those elements of treatment immediately essential to secure the child's welfare should be given. Other non-urgent treatment should be delayed while the local authority consider bringing an application in care proceedings. If an interim order is made in these proceedings, this transfers parental rights to the authority, enabling them to give consent. If this course is inappropriate, wardship may be the proper response.

As for the converse position, where the parents ask for the child to be examined by their own doctor, since the parental right to consent to medical treatment survives a place of safety order, the local authority should in principle allow the doctor to see the child. Access could be denied on the basis that a further examination would harm the child or the authority may be spurred into seeking an interim order immediately.

3.3 The Primary Conditions

Under the CYPA 1969, s. 1 (2), a child can be brought before a court in care proceedings where it is alleged that:

(a) his proper development is being avoidably prevented or neglected or his health is being avoidably impaired or neglected or he is being ill-treated; or

(b)   it is probable that the condition set out in the preceding paragraph will be satisfied in his case, having regard to the fact that the court or another court has found that that condition is or was satisfied in the case of another child or young person who is or was a member of the household to which he belongs; or

(bb) it is probable that the conditions set out in para. (*a*) will be satisfied in his case, having regard to the fact that a person who has been convicted of an offence mentioned in Sch. 1 to the Children and Young Persons Act 1933, including a person convicted of such an offence on whose conviction for the offence an order was made under Part I of the Powers of Criminal Courts Act 1973 placing him on probation or discharging him absolutely or conditionally is, or may become, a member of the same household as the child; or

(c)   he is exposed to moral danger; or

(d)   he is beyond the control of his parent or guardian; or

(e)   he is of compulsory school age within the meaning of the Education Act 1944 and is not receiving efficient full-time education suitable to his age, ability and aptitude and to any special educational needs he may have; or

(f)   he is guilty of an offence, excluding homicide.

3.4 Paragraph (a)

The child's proper development is being avoidably prevented or neglected or his health is being avoidably impaired or neglected or he is being ill-treated. While para. (*a*) is expressed as a single condition it may be satisfied by evidence of one of five circumstances, namely:

(1) the child's proper development is being avoidably prevented;
(2) the child's proper development is being avoidably neglected;
(3) the child's health is being avoidably impaired;
(4) the child's health is being avoidably neglected;
(5) the child is being ill-treated

However, for the purpose of drafting the notice of complaint, it is not necessary to specify which circumstance is being alleged. It is sufficient if the notice makes it clear that in substance para. (*a*) is being relied upon, *Wooley* v *Haines* (1976) 140 JP 16.

3.4.1 Standards

The scope of para. (*a*) is broad and the standards to be applied to each of its parts is unclear. In care proceedings there is often a very difficult balance to be struck between allowing parents to bring up their own child as they see fit, and protecting a child against inadequate, incompetent, improper or cruel forms of care or control. The burden of setting standards falls initially on the local authority or the NSPCC. They must decide whether there appears to be grounds for taking care proceedings. Usually this involves an assessment of how much risk to the child is acceptable, and whether the provision of social work support, assistance and services (and exceptionally cash as authorized under s. 1 of the Child Care Act 1980 (CCA)) will afford adequate protection to the child. In practice the degrees of risk acceptable to local authorities would sometimes appear to vary according to whether the child comes from a deprived inner city area or from a more prosperous rural community. In care proceedings there is a tension between the child, the parents and the State as protector of the child. For example, when does severe punishment of a child amount to ill-treatment in a society which permits corporal punishment? Evidence which may satisfy one court that there are grounds for intervention may fail to satisfy another, and the decision of the court reflects society's unpredictable norms on the care and control of children.

The question becomes aggravated when the child before the court comes from a different culture, and where the expectations and responses of the parents are alien to the 'English way of life'. It has been held, in the context of wardship, that where the court is dealing with a wholly different culture, the basic responsibility of the court remains, namely to apply English law. The court must consider the case against the reasonable objective standards of the culture in which the children have hitherto been brought up, so long as these do not conflict with the minimal acceptable standards of child care in England. But there may well be circumstances where a society from which the child comes lays down standards of conduct that wholly offend against the canons and principles of English society, for example, chastisement with sticks of a nature and to a degree which are unacceptable, see *Re H (A Minor)* [1987] 2 FLR 12.

In a few cases society has made it clear that it will not tolerate different cultural practices, and a local authority is entitled to intervene (see Prohibition of Female Circumcision Act 1985; prohibition of marriage in England under the age of sixteen, Marriage Act 1949). In many others toleration prevails, but underlying tension can occasionally surface. For example, the British-born daughter of Asian or Middle Eastern immigrants may rebel against an arranged marriage or system of purdah imposed by her parents. Whether a local authority is prepared to intervene to assist the child, and to argue before a juvenile court that this amounts to ill-treatment, or the prevention of the child's proper development, will depend greatly on its race relations policy.

If parental rights are not to be unnecessarily infringed, then a child's 'proper' development cannot mean his optimal development, but must instead mean compliance with a minimum acceptable standard. For example, this standard may not be reached where a baby is failing to thrive or a toddler to grow at the rate expected. Paragraph (*a*) covers a range of situations such as assaults, sexual abuse, mental cruelty, parental inadequacy or parental indifference which are manifested in physical or psychological damage to the child. The task of proving this can be extremely difficult. In some cases the evidence will be clear (for example, cigarette burns on the child), but even with physical injuries explanations may be proffered (for example that the child broke his arm by falling accidentally down the stairs, or that his burns were caused by falling against an electric fire) which have to be resolved by detailed expert evidence or by thorough cross-examination of parents. A particularly valuable indicator of harm to young child is the percentile chart which is used to record a child's weight and then to compare it with the range of weights which should be expected of a child of the same age.

It has been held that a child's proper development and health includes his emotional development and health, *F* v *Suffolk CC* (1981) 2 FLR 208. Normally the harm caused to the child is established by medical evidence, but this is not essential. In *F* v *Suffolk CC* (above) justices heard evidence from an experienced social worker and health visitor. It was held that they did not need to have heard psychiatric evidence to justify their finding that the child's mental development was being impaired or neglected. In most cases, however, where there is no evidence of physical damage to the child, but where mental or emotional damage is alleged, expert (and frequently conflicting) evidence will be required and the court will be faced with the acute problem of determining the proper standard to apply.

3.4.2. 'Avoidably'

'Avoidably' lends itself to two opposing interpretations. On the one hand, it means that there are grounds for intervention only when those who are causing harm to the child could avoid doing so by an effort of will. This interpretation leads to the undesirable result that an application must be dismissed where the parent, because of a physical or mental disability, cannot avoid treating the child in a damaging fashion, and this reasoning led magistrates to discharge a care order in *Salford CC* v *C* (1982) 3 FLR 153 (the High Court, hearing the case in wardship, gave no ruling on the point).

The alternative view is that 'avoidably' means that harm to the child can be avoided if he is treated differently, regardless of culpability. It is suggested that this is the correct interpretation. The focus of care proceedings is on the condition of the child, and whilst this will often require proof of culpability in the parent, it should not be essential. Where the child is being harmed and where the parent cannot 'avoid' what he is doing, an order is necessary if the child is to be protected.

3.4.3 Present tense drafting

It should be noted that this ground for care proceedings is phrased in the present tense, and makes no reference either to the past or to future events. But where a child is being neglected or ill-treated he is often removed from home for several weeks before the final hearing. Thus, typically, a place of safety order is followed by an interim order, and then further interim orders to enable the child's guardian ad litem to complete his inquiries. By the time of the trial the child may have fully recovered from his treatment. The courts have interpreted the present tense drafting of para. (*a*) realistically and have refused to countenance the argument that, where the child is currently being properly looked after, the ground cannot be proved. They have taken this view not only when the child is presently living, for example, in a community home or with foster-parents, but also where he has been placed back at home with his parents although the subject of an interim order, and where he has not come to harm during the period immediately preceding the final hearing, *M* v *Westminster CC* [1985] FLR 325. It has been stated that the development of a child is a continuing matter, and encompasses the past, the present and, to a certain extent, the future. The words 'is being' indicate a situation over a period of time sufficiently proximate to the date of the court hearing to indicate that it is the present and continuing set of circumstances which is descriptive of the child's condition, *F* v *Suffolk CC* (1981) 2 FLR 208; *M* v *Westminster CC* (above). This construction was endorsed by the House of Lords in *Re D (A Minor)* [1987] 1 FLR 422. Furthermore, it was held that the court, in considering whether a continuing situation of one or other of the kinds described in s. 1 (2) (*a*) exists, must do so at the point of time immediately before the process of protecting the child concerned is first put into motion (see also *H* v *Sheffield CC* (1982)

JSWL 303). In *Re D (A Minor)* (above) a child was born suffering from drug withdrawal symptoms. She was kept in hospital and never allowed into the care of her mother. It was found that the prevention and impairment of the child's development and health had been caused by the mother's excessive drug-taking while the child was in her womb, and that the child, since birth, had never been out of the care of responsible agencies. It was held by the House of Lords that the juvenile court is entitled to look back to the period before the child was born when considering whether the condition specified in s. 1 (2) (*a*) is established, and that the legislative purpose is best furthered in a case of this kind by allowing such an approach.

On the other hand, s. 1 (2) (*a*) does not cover fear of future harm where none has already occurred, no matter how imminent the threatened harm may be, *Essex CC* v *TLR and KBR (Minors)* (1979) 9 Fam. Law 15. This view was endorsed in *Re D (A Minor)*, but with the caveat that the *Essex* case must not be regarded as good authority for the wider proposition that it is never permissible for the court to look at the hypothetical future. It can do so provided it is in conjunction with the present and the past. However, difficulties can arise, for example, where the child's mother or father develops a serious mental disorder, or where a severely physically or mentally handicapped woman gives birth to a child, or where a surrogate mother plans to hand the newborn child to the couple who have used her services, or where a man believed to be dangerous joins the household. The proper and most satisfactory response to these and similar circumstances is for the local authority to institute wardship proceedings (see chapter 6).

3.5 Paragraph (b)

It is probable that the condition set out in para. (a) will be satisfied having regard to the fact that the court or another court has found that para. (a) is or was satisfied in the case of another child who is or was a member of the household to which the child before the court belongs.

The essence of para. (*b*) is that it enables the court to make an order where there is a risk of harm, rather than where harm has already occurred. It is this paragraph which authorizes the removal of siblings from the home when one child has been neglected or ill-treated, and which enables a local authority to seek an order in respect of a newborn baby. Sometimes fear for other children in the household arises because one child has already been killed. Where this happens para. (*b*) can still apply, see *Surrey CC* v *S* [1974] QB 124 where the court was satisfied that para. (*a*) would have been satisfied in respect of the dead child (although in such a case the notice of proceedings should specifically state that the court will be asked to find para. (*a*) proved).

3.5.1 Household

It must be established that the child, to whom para. (*a*) applies, is or was a member of the household to which the child presently before the court belongs. In determining the meaning of 'household' the court must have regard to the persons comprising its membership, not its locality. In *N (A Minor)* v *Birmingham DC* (1984) 128 SJ 447 a mother had two children; the first was in care under the CYPA 1969 before the second was born. The mother had left her husband, the father of the first child, and set up house with another man who fathered her second child. It was held in the Divisional Court that the older child was a member of the second household because the mother was the dominant member. This wide interpretation of household makes it easier for proceedings to be brought in respect of a child believed to be at risk from one member of the family, when its other members have altered, and where a new family unit has been set up.

3.6 Paragraph (bb)

It is probable that the condition set out in para. (a) will be satisfied having regard to the fact that a person who has been convicted of an offence mentioned in Sch. 1 to the Children and Young Persons Act 1933 is, or may become, a member of the same household as the child before the court.

This paragraph, like para. (*b*), enables the court to make an order where a child is believed to be at risk of harm. The offences referred to are murder, manslaughter, infanticide, other offences of wounding or causing bodily injury, sexual offences and any other offence involving bodily injury to a child or young person. In each case the victim of the offence must have been a child or young person. Conviction for the purposes of para. (*bb*) includes a finding of guilt which resulted in a probation order or an absolute or conditional discharge.

This paragraph can be relied on when the convicted person 'may become' a member of the same household as the child and this allows swift intervention even before the convicted person has joined the household, for example, because he is due to be released from prison. However, it should be noted that the child cannot be protected under this ground where the offence has been committed against an adult, however dangerous the convicted person may appear to be. In these circumstances the child should be made a ward of court.

3.7 Paragraph (c)

The child is exposed to moral danger. In this more than the other paragraphs, much can depend on the practitioner's experience of the local juvenile court's persuasions. The phrase 'moral danger' covers the whole of a child's environment, such as where a girl starts to engage in prostitution, or a young boy becomes involved in a homosexual relationship with a much older man, or where the child is being exposed to moral danger by the adults who are caring for him. Paragraph (*c*) is primarily, though not necessarily, linked with sexual activity in the young. Sometimes it is relied upon, in conjunction with para. (*d*) (the child is beyond control), where a girl is having sexual intercourse below the age of consent (sixteen) and the parents are unable to control her behaviour. Where a child is living in a household in which the adult members encourage him to join in with their sexual activities, or where he is regularly taken out shoplifting, or encouraged to burgle houses, or to take drugs, this paragraph can also apply. These examples fall squarely within 'moral danger', but inevitably there are others where the paragraph's imprecision will be exposed.

It has been held in a case involving immigrants from Nigeria that in assessing whether a child is in moral danger the standards of 'English people' and the 'English way of life' should not be rigidly applied to people from other cultures, where the behaviour in issue would be acceptable in the foreign country in which the parties have been brought up, *Alhaji Mohamed* v *Knott* [1969] 1 QB 1. However, there must be limits to this approach when public policy and repugnance so dictate. Furthermore, it is suggested that where the sexual activity to which the immigrant child is exposed appears to put the child's health and development at risk, the proper course is for proceedings to be instituted under para. (*a*). Thus, sexual intercourse between a pre-pubertal thirteen-year-old girl and her husband who suffers from a venereal disease (the facts of *Alhaji Mohamed* v *Knott* (above)) may not expose the girl to moral danger, but it could seriously damage her health. This course of action also has the clear advantage that proof of para. (*a*) is usually much easier than proof of para. (*c*).

3.8 Paragraph (d)

The child is beyond the control of his parent or guardian. This ground differs from the others, in that not only can the proceedings be instigated by the usual applicants (the local authority, the NSPCC or the police) but also the parent is given an independent right to request the local authority to initiate proceedings. If the local authority refuse to comply with this request, the parent can apply to a juvenile court for an order requiring them to do so, CYPA 1963, s. 3 (1).

3.8.1 Liberty of the child

Whether a child is beyond the control of his parent is a matter of fact, but it is suggested that the breakdown in parental control should be serious before compulsory intervention by a court is warranted. If the court makes a care order or a supervision order then the liberty of that child is directly affected. Teenagers, notoriously, can be disruptive, disobedient, and difficult to live with. Whether this behaviour justifies a court order, often leading to institutional care, is a matter of degree. But a balance must be maintained between allowing a parent to rid himself of the responsibility for a difficult and uncontrollable teenager, and the right of the child to remain in his own home.

3.8.2 Children under ten

Section 50 of the CYPA 1933 states 'it shall be conclusively presumed that no child under the age of ten years can be guilty of any offence'. This provision safeguards children from being prosecuted and punished by courts under the age of ten because, as a matter of law, they are incapable of having the guilty mind to be criminally liable for their acts. Nonetheless it has been stated that para. (*d*) 'is more likely to be invoked where children are troublesome but cannot be proved to have committed offences, perhaps because they are under the age of ten' (*Parents and Children* by Brenda Hoggett, p. 87). It is suggested that great caution should be exercised before reliance is placed on the 'beyond control' ground in these circumstances. There may be some extreme cases where the parents are at their "wits' end" and intervention under para. (*d*) is appropriate, but even then reception into care under s. 2 of the CCA 1980 is preferable. Where it is the police who make the application, then taking care proceedings becomes almost tantamount to authorizing the prosecution of non-offenders. In a case where a parent encourages or acquiesces in a young child 'offending' it may be that proceedings can be brought on the ground that his proper development is being avoidably prevented, para. (*a*), or that he is exposed to moral danger, para. (*c*).

3.8.3 Legal representation of the child

When a child is brought before the court on the ground that he is beyond the control of his parent, the parent is prohibited from representing him, CYP Rules 1988, r. 22 (1). Independent legal representation for the child would appear to be essential in order to safeguard his position and this should be ordered by the court. Sometimes it may also be desirable that a guardian ad litem is appointed (see §4.1.1)

3.9 Paragraph (e)

The child is of compulsory school age and is not receiving efficient full-time education suitable to his age, ability and aptitude and to any special educational needs he may have. Care proceedings for non-attendance at school should be looked at in conjunction with the powers available to a local education authority to prosecute parents for failing to send their child to school under the Education Act 1944. Before bringing a prosecution the local authority are under a duty to consider care proceedings as an alternative to prosecuting the parents, Education Act 1944, s. 40 (2). An application under para. (*e*) is usually made when a child persists in truancy despite efforts made by his parents, teachers, education welfare officers and social workers to secure his attendance at school. It is often made as a last resort.

Section 2 (8) (*b*) of the CYPA 1969 provides that condition (*e*) shall be deemed to be satisfied if the child is aged between five and sixteen, and it is proved that he:

(1) is the subject of a school attendance order under s. 37 of the Education Act 1944 which has not been complied with; or
(2) is a registered pupil at a school which he is not attending regularly within the meaning of s. 39 of the 1944 Act; or
(3) is a person whom another person habitually wandering from place to place takes with him.

Regular attendance is not defined and local education authorities set different standards of attendance according to the age and circumstances of the child, before any action is taken.

In *Re S (A Minor) (Care Order: Education)* [1978] QB 120 the question was raised whether a well-behaved, well-disciplined and respectful boy aged twelve, who was not being sent to school because his parents had an implacable objection to comprehensive education, could be made the subject of a care order. It should be remembered that an applicant in care proceedings must prove both limbs of s. 1 (2) of the CYPA 1969, namely that the child is in one or more of the specified conditions *and* that he is in need of care or control which he is unlikely to receive unless the court makes an order. It was held by the Court of Appeal that a child who is not receiving a proper education is in need of care within the meaning of the CYPA 1969, and that magistrates had been correct to make a care order. Thus proof of the primary condition in para. (*e*) can in itself satisfy both limbs of the application.

3.9.1 Adjourning the hearing

In some juvenile courts the practice has grown up of adjourning the application at the end of the hearing of an education case. The court may wish for a period of time to elapse between finding the application proved and deciding which order to make (normally the choice lies between a care order or a supervision order). Often the court uses the period of adjournment as a mechanism for attempting to secure the child's proper attendance at school. The magistrates warn the child that should he fail to attend school during the adjournment period, then he is liable to be put into care. Some magistrates bring the child back repeatedly before their court in order to monitor his progress, but without making any order. It is doubtful whether these repeated adjournments are a proper use of the court's powers. The court has already decided that an order is necessary when finding the case proved. It is entitled to adjourn before deciding what order to make, but not to use this power for some ulterior purpose.

3.10 Paragraph (f)

The child is guilty of an offence, excluding homicide. The offence condition is relied on rarely. In 1983 only thirteen applications were made under this paragraph, and this figure reflects similar numbers in the preceding years. Although the proceedings are civil, the standard of proof is beyond reasonable doubt because an offence is alleged. Only if the offence is proved can the court consider the second limb in care proceedings, namely whether the child is in need of care or control. At this stage the standard of proof reverts to the civil standard. In addition to those orders which can be made on proof of one of the other conditions (see §4.6), a compensation order can be made; also a recognizance order for good behaviour is possible, CYPA 1969, s. 3 (6), (7).

3.11 Overriding Condition: Care or Control

The court must be satisfied that one or more of the seven specified primary conditions apply to the child, and also that the child 'is in need of care or control which he is unlikely to receive unless the court makes an order'. Care includes protection and guidance, and control includes discipline, CYPA 1969, s. 70 (1). The care or control provision is a forward-looking test; the court is required to consider what will happen to the child if an order is, or is not, made. It does not necessarily follow from proof of one of the primary conditions that a court order is the only means of providing the child with proper care or control. For example, a voluntary arrangement could be made between the parents and the local authority for the child to be received into care under the CCA 1980, s. 2; or a relative could offer to look after the child (see chapter 7).

An important consideration here is whether, looking to the future, the local authority consider it to be essential to have parental rights over the child. This may pose a dilemma, because if a child is admitted into care voluntarily, and it later becomes clear that a compulsory order is needed, the opportunity to obtain such an order may have been lost. It may be the case that at this stage there are no longer grounds for instituting care proceedings, because of the present tense drafting of several of the primary conditions (though see §3.4.3). Although the care and control provision is an additional matter which the applicant must prove, in practice if the primary condition is satisfied then the court will normally be satisfied that it needs to make an order in respect of the child. It may, however, be persuaded that a supervision order will afford the child proper care or control in an appropriate case.

4 CARE PROCEEDINGS: THE HEARING

4.1 Legal Representation of the Child

At the outset of care proceedings a decision must be made as to whether a parent should be allowed to represent the child in the proceedings. Rule 22 of the CYP Rules 1988 provides that the court must allow the parent to conduct the case on the child's behalf unless either the child or his parent is legally represented, or the proceedings are brought at the parent's request on the ground that the child is beyond control, or an order has been made under the CYPA 1969, s. 32A (see below), or the child objects. Allowing a parent to represent his child is clearly appropriate where the interests of the child and those of the parent coincide. However, it is often not clear whether their interests coincide or conflict; for example, even where an application for a care order is unopposed by the parent, the making of such an order is not necessarily in the best interests of the child (cf. the facts of *W* v *Hertfordshire CC* [1985] FLR 879). Section 32A (1) of the CYPA 1969 provides that if before or in the course of care proceedings it appears to the court that there is or may be a conflict between the interests of the child and those of his parent, the court may order that the parent is not to be treated as representing the child. Because of the nature of the grounds for an application in care proceedings (see chapter 3), and because the court need only be satisfied that there *may* be a conflict of interests, it is suggested that in principle an order should be made in the majority of cases. For it does not matter that the local authority will support the child's interests; s. 32A speaks only of a conflict between the child and the parents.

Courts differ widely on the procedures they adopt when making an order under s. 32A. Some hold a formal preliminary hearing before a bench of three justices, allow the parent to be legally represented and determine the issue in a formal judicial manner. Others arrange for a representative of the local authority to speak in private to a single justice who then determines the issue (in this case

57

a juvenile court deputy chairman would be the most appropriate person). In some courts the order is made by the justices' clerk, after consultation with the local authority.

It has been held that while the making of an order under s. 32(A) (1) is a judicial act, it can nonetheless be made *ex parte*. There is no breach of the rules of natural justice if the parents are not heard before the order is made, see *R* v *Plymouth Juvenile Court ex parte F and F* [1987] 1 FLR 169. But it was suggested in the *Plymouth* case that it would help to avoid uncertainty if notice of any order made under s. 32A is given to any persons entitled to be notified of the proceedings under r. 14. This suggestion has since been implemented in r. 15 of the 1988 Rules. The form of notice sent to the parent tells him that he has been made a party to the proceedings and has a right to take part in them on his own behalf (see §4.2). It was further suggested in the *Plymouth* case that it would be helpful if such notice indicated what decisions had been made as to the appointment of a guardian ad litem and a lawyer for the child. The rules are silent on this, but notification could be adopted as a matter of good practice.

4.1.1 Appointment and duties of a guardian ad litem of the child

Where the court makes an order under s. 32A (1) it must appoint a guardian ad litem of the child if it appears to the court that it is in the child's interests to do so, CYP Rules 1988, r. 16 (1). In the majority of cases this will be so. Nonetheless this safeguard for the child is frequently absent in some parts of the country where, through lack of resources, there is a grave shortage of guardians ad litem. In other parts the shortage may mean a considerable delay before a guardian ad litem can be found. In *R* v *Plymouth Juvenile Court ex parte F and F* (above) some guidance was given to juvenile courts on when they should appoint a guardian ad litem in the face of such a shortage. It was stated that a solicitor would benefit from the independent view of an experienced guardian ad litem in a case where he is acting on behalf of an infant too young to give instructions. For here he is likely to have limited opportunities to make close, independent investigations of the facts and circumstances. He thus may feel obliged to support the local authority's case unless he has recourse to that independent view.

The guardian ad litem has various duties. One of these is to obtain the views of the court as to whether the child should be legally represented and, unless the court otherwise directs, to instruct a solicitor to represent the child, r. 16 (6) (c). Alternatively the court, a single justice or the justices' clerk can order that the child is legally represented when the guardian ad litem is initially appointed, r. 16 (4). The guardian ad litem has a duty to consider how the case should be presented on behalf of the child, acting in conjunction with the child's solicitor. The solicitor takes his instructions from the guardian ad litem, and their joint duty is to safeguard the interests of the child before the court. The guardian ad litem is given specific investigative duties: he must interview such persons, inspect such records and obtain such professional assistance as he thinks appropriate. This puts the child's solicitor in an unusual position, as normally he would engage in these activities on behalf of his client. The rules envisage that the guardian ad litem and the solicitor will co-operate in preparing the child's case; for their team-work to be effective the solicitor's legal skills should complement the guardian ad litem's social work skills. In particular the solicitor should discuss with the guardian ad litem the type of evidence to be presented to the court and whether the solicitor too should interview witnesses, either alone or in the company of the guardian ad litem. (On evidence generally, see chapter 1.) The child's solicitor should, throughout, be conscious that it is the child who is his client, albeit that he is instructed by the guardian ad litem, and he should note that the report of the panel of inquiry into the circumstances surrounding the death of Jasmine Beckford (1985) recommends that any solicitor acting for a child in care proceedings should see, and if possible talk to or play with, the child. However, sometimes this may be disturbing for the child for he may already have been visited, spoken to and questioned by a number of strange adults, so it is important to consult the guardian ad litem about this.

When representing the interests of the child before the court the guardian ad litem must regard as the first and paramount consideration the need to safeguard and promote the child's best interests until he achieves adulthood. He must also take account of the child's wishes and feelings, having regard to his age and understanding, and he must ensure that those wishes and feelings are made known to the court, r. 16 (6) (*b*). Sometimes the wishes and feelings of the child will conflict with the guardian ad litem's assessment of his own best interests. For example, the guardian ad litem believes that the child's best interests will be served if a care order is made; the child, on the other hand, does not want to go into care. Where this occurs, and where, having regard to his age and understanding, the child wishes and is able to give instructions on his own behalf which conflict with those of the guardian ad litem, the solicitor must take the child's instructions, r. 16 (6) (*d*). But this does not always mean that the solicitor and the guardian ad litem must part company throughout the proceedings. For it may be that the child's instructions differ from those of the guardian ad litem only as regards the method of disposal, the child wishing for a supervision order, the guardian ad litem recommending a care order. Here the solicitor can join with the guardian in supporting proof of the primary ground and part company only with respect to the order proposed. To avoid confusion the solicitor is advised to explain to the court at the outset of the case when he is instructed by the child and when by the guardian ad litem.

4.2 Legal Representation of the Parent

A parent must be notified of an application made in care proceedings if his whereabouts are known or can readily be ascertained by the applicant, CYP Rules 1988, r. 14 (3) (*b*). (For the meaning of 'parent', see §7.5.1.) A parent has the right to attend the hearing as a person directly concerned in the case, and indeed he can be compelled to attend by the court, Children and Young Persons Act 1933 (CYPA), ss. 47 (2) and 34 (1). A parent is entitled to be legally represented, but he is not entitled to legal aid to be separately represented where his child is being legally represented, unless the court makes an order under s. 32A of the CYPA 1969 disqualifying him from representing the child, Legal Aid Act 1974, s. 28 (6A) (see further on legal aid, §1.9). Where such an order is made, the parent automatically becomes a party to the proceedings, CYPA 1969, s. 32A (4A).

4.2.1 The parent's rights in the proceedings

The parent who is not a party is given rights under the rules which are technically narrower than those enjoyed by a party to the proceedings. Rule 18 states that the parent is entitled:

(a) to meet any allegations made against him in the course of the proceedings by cross-examining any witness and calling or giving evidence; and
(b) to make representations to the court.

A parent who is a party is not limited to exercising these rights, but can call evidence and cross-examine witnesses on any matters which are relevant to the proceedings. In practice many courts adopt the approach of treating the parent as if he is a party to the proceedings whatever his technical status.

4.2.2 Discovering the applicant's case

The only formal disclosure to the parent of the applicant's case is the notice served under r. 14 specifying the grounds for the application, and the names and addresses of the persons to whom a copy of the notice has been sent. To prepare his case properly, the parent needs to know in advance of the hearing the nature of any allegations to be made against him. The formal notice will not specify them and it will often be unclear what allegations are being made about the condition of the child. For example, s. 1 (2) (*a*) of the CYPA 1969 states that the child's 'proper development is being avoidably prevented or neglected or his health is being avoidably impaired or neglected or he is being ill-treated'. But the notice will not tell the parent whether the applicant's concern is for the child's proper development or his health, or whether he is allegedly being neglected or ill-treated. Such limited notification is inadequate, and may breach the rule of natural justice that a person has the right to know the case which is being made against him. Accordingly, the parent has the right to demand that the applicant gives him detailed notice of the allegations being made, including, possibly, copies of the statements of witnesses, *R* v *West Malling Juvenile Court ex parte K* [1986] 2 FLR 405.

If at any stage the question arises whether a disqualifying order should be made under s. 32A (1) of the CYPA 1969, this can be a useful occasion for clarifying the position of all people concerned in the proceedings. Where the parent has approached a solicitor before any such order has been made, the solicitor is well advised to make a request to the justices' clerk that he and his client should attend at court when either the justices or their clerk are considering whether to disqualify the parent from representing his child. The nature of the alleged conflict of interests between the child and his parent will normally be disclosed by the applicant during these proceedings (see §1.6 on privileged information).

Another important source of information is the guardian ad litem's report. In the absence of special circumstances this must be made available to the parties, parents and certainly their legal advisers as early as possible, and well in advance of the hearing, *R* v *Epsom Juvenile Court ex parte G* [1988] 1 All ER 329. This prior disclosure not only accords with natural justice but also reduces the possibility of subsequent adjournments. However, the guardian ad litem's report cannot be disclosed to anyone other than these persons (for example, a social worker whom the parents wish to instruct) without the court's permission, *R* v *Sunderland Juvenile Court ex parte G* [1988] 2 FLR 40.

4.3 Interim Orders

When the court is not in the position to decide what order, if any, it ought to make, it can make an interim order in respect of the child, CYPA 1969, s. 2 (10). This commits the child to the care of the local authority for a maximum period of 28 days. The court has no power to order where the child will live during the period of the interim order, and cannot attach any conditions to the order, *Re Jarvis (Minors)* [1984] FLR 350.

The applicant is not required to discharge any burden of proof before an interim order is made. There are no statutory criteria for making or refusing to make an order. However, it was stated in *R v Croydon Juvenile Court ex parte N* [1987] 1 FLR 252 that the magistrates must have before them sufficient reliable material on which they can exercise their discretion judicially as to the making of an interim order. Practice between courts varies: some require the local authority to prove that there are reasonable grounds for believing that one of the conditions in s. 1 (2) (*a*)–(*e*) of the CYPA 1969 applies to the child; others are prepared to make an order after hearing only very limited evidence. Where an application for an interim order is opposed by the parent, evidence must be presented and the parent must be afforded the opportunity to challenge this evidence in the manner specified in r. 18, namely to meet any allegations made against him by cross-examining any witness, calling or giving evidence and making representations to the court, *R v Croydon Juvenile Court ex parte N* (above); *R v Birmingham Juvenile Court ex parte Birmingham CC* [1988] 1 WLR 337. The difficulty here lies in ensuring natural justice to the parent on the one hand and avoiding unduly lengthy hearings on the other, for often several interim orders are sought to enable the guardian ad litem to complete his report. It is here that the lawyers must exercise their skill and good sense, trying wherever possible to agree the evidence (for witnesses with other duties cannot reasonably be expected to appear at several successive hearings). However, where a parent wishes to oppose each application the court must allow evidence to be presented and permit the parent to test that evidence, *R v Birmingham Juvenile Court ex parte N* [1984] FLR 683. Thus co-operation and compromise between the lawyers are essential.

It has frequently been emphasized that a local authority have a duty to deal expeditiously with care proceedings. Delay sometimes occurs while an adult is being prosecuted for an offence against the child. In this case the child's solicitor, mindful that delay can be prejudicial to the child's welfare, may wish to draw the court's attention both to Home Office Circular 84/1982, which states that care proceedings should not automatically be adjourned where there is no reason to believe that they will prejudice the trial, for example, when the defendant intends to plead guilty, and to the decision of Sir Stephen Brown in *R v Exeter Juvenile Court ex parte H*; *R v Waltham Forest Juvenile Court ex parte B* (1988) *The Times*, February 19. Here parents had submitted that care proceedings should be adjourned because they would be prejudiced by them in the subsequent criminal proceedings. In an important ruling, the President stated that the guiding principle for the juvenile court is the paramountcy of the child's welfare, and that delay should be avoided. Again in *R v Inner London Juvenile Court ex parte G* [1988] 2 FLR 58, the child had already been in care for three months and was showing signs of disturbed behaviour. The guardian ad litem was very keen for the early disposal of the case, and an adjournment pending trial of the father would have led to a further delay of four months. It was held that the juvenile court was quite justified in refusing the father's request for an adjournment, and in proceeding to a final hearing. If an adjournment request is granted the local authority may advisedly consider wardship, where it may better be recognized that 'the court is not trying the parents in the sense of trying an allegation of a criminal offence, it is assessing the needs of the court's ward', *Re P (A Minor)* [1987] 2 FLR 467 (per Stephen Brown LJ).

4.3.1 Presence of the child

Children under the age of five or those prevented by illness or accident need not attend any hearings for an interim order, CYPA 1969, s. 22 (1) (*b*). As for older children, they must attend on the first application for an interim order, but the court may then direct that the child need not be brought before the court on subsequent applications provided the child is legally represented, CYPA 1969, s. 22 (2) (see too *Northamptonshire CC v H* [1988] 1 FLR 529). This is a useful safeguard for the child, who can be spared what is often an ordeal. The attention of the justices should be brought to this provision so that the appropriate direction can be made.

4.3.2 Withdrawal of the application

Once an application has been commenced in care proceedings it cannot be withdrawn without the leave of the court. Before granting such leave the justices should be presented with submissions upon which they can exercise their discretion judicially (for example, new evidence has come to light since the last interim hearing). It was stated in *R* v *Birmingham Juvenile Court ex parte G*; *R* v *Birmingham Juvenile Court ex parte R* (1988) *The Independent*, May 10, that a local authority should never apply to withdraw proceedings without first fully consulting with the guardian ad litem who represents the child. Furthermore, in a case where the guardian ad litem wishes the application to continue, the court must allow him to call evidence and to place his report before the court. It was emphasized that it is wrong for a local authority formally to offer no evidence when the guardian ad litem opposes the withdrawal.

4.3.3 Discharge by the High Court

The child may apply to the High Court for an interim order to be discharged. The court may discharge the order on such terms as it thinks fit, but where it refuses to do so the court may further order the local authority not to place the child in the charge of a parent or other person except with the consent and in accordance with any directions of the High Court. The child's application will succeed only where he can show that the justices acted mistakenly on the facts, or on the basis of a wrong principle of law, or that their decision was plainly wrong, *R* v *Birmingham Juvenile Court ex parte N* [1984] FLR 683.

4.4 Attendance at the Hearing

The following persons have a *prima facie* right to attend a hearing in care proceedings: members and officers of the court; parties to the case, their lawyers, witnesses and other persons directly concerned in the case; *bona fide* representatives of the press; and any such persons as the court may specifically authorize, CYPA 1933, s. 47 (2). This right is qualified by the court's inherent jurisdiction to exclude any such person. However, the following persons should be excluded only in the most exceptional circumstances: any party to the proceedings, or his legal representative; the social worker or other person in practical charge of the case for the local authority; and any expert witness proposed to be called to give evidence. Furthermore, the social worker or other person in practical charge should normally be present throughout the proceedings and there is no general principle that witnesses should be excluded from the court before they give evidence. An exclusion order can be made only if an application has been made to the justices. They, in reaching their decision, must consider all the circumstances. In some cases a witness's testimony might be improperly affected if he remains in court. In others, his presence may assist a party or the court or may prevent the unnecessary duplication of evidence, *R* v *Willesden Justices ex parte Brent LB* [1988] 2 FLR 95. Two types of exclusion call for special comment, as follows.

4.4.1 Excluding the child from the court

The court has the power to hear the whole or part of the evidence in the child's absence where it believes this to be in the child's interests, unless the child is conducting his own case, r. 23 (1). In many cases it will be sensible for the court to address itself to this question before the case commences. In order to make an informed decision the court will need to rely on the lawyers present alerting the court to potentially damaging evidence, so that it can protect the child from the trauma of hearing certain information, or of witnessing conflict in cross-examination. A lawyer should remember that the court has no prior knowledge of the case. In particular it does not know what type of evidence a witness intends to give. For this reason he should use his initiative in drawing the court's attention to the distressing nature of some of the evidence, and should suggest that the court might like to exercise its power to exclude the child.

Evidence relating to the child's character or conduct must be heard in his presence, r. 23 (1). It is unlikely that a court would give too literal an interpretation to this provision, as this would be to undermine the wider purpose of the rule which is to protect the child's welfare. Thus, evidence about a child's disturbed behaviour, allegedly arising as a result of neglect or ill-treatment, could properly be heard in his absence. But where specific allegations are being made against the child, such as that he is not going to school, or is beyond his parent's control, he should be present in the court. A balance must be struck between protecting the child and allowing him to hear and deal with allegations made against him. In cases of doubt it may be that the presence of the guardian ad litem and the child's lawyer will afford adequate protection of his interests (cf. *Northamptonshire CC* v *H* [1988] 1 FLR 529).

4.4.2 Excluding the parents and other persons from the court

The court may require the parents and other persons to withdraw from the court while the child gives evidence or makes a statement, provided that it informs such a person of the substance of any allegations made against him by the child, r. 23 (2). The child may find it easier to express himself freely, or to make allegations against his parents or others if they are not listening. The child's lawyer should consider whether to discuss this with the child before the hearing. In any event, it must be made clear to the child that the court cannot treat what he says as confidential to the court, and that, where the child has made allegations against a person, the court is under a duty to tell that person of the substance of these allegations so that he has the opportunity to deny them.

4.5 Conduct of the Case

Rules 14 and 16 (1) of the Magistrates' Courts Rules 1981, which designate the order of evidence and speeches and the form of order, apply to care proceedings as if they were by way of complaint. However, because the parent (and occasionally a third party) has a right to be heard in the proceedings, and because the guardian ad litem has an independent right to give evidence, these rules have been extended by the CYP Rules 1988 to accommodate all these interested persons.

4.5.1 Order of speeches

At the outset the court must explain to the child or, if he is absent or too young, to his parent, the general nature of the proceedings and the grounds on which they are brought. If orders have been made under ss. 32A or 32C, a parent or a grandparent may be a party and the court needs to consider how the proceedings should be conducted. Unfortunately the CYP Rules 1988 are both unclear and unhelpful. They make complex provision for the order of proceedings and, if strictly observed, the following procedure operates:

(1) The applicant's lawyer opens the case. If he wishes he can first address the court. If he intends to make a final address to the court, it is good practice to alert the court at this stage. He then calls his witnesses who can be cross-examined, first by a grandparent (if made a party to the proceedings), second, by a parent (if similarly a party) and third, by the child's lawyer. If the parent is not a party to the proceedings, his cross-examination is technically restricted to meeting allegations made against him (though the court may permit him a fuller role). In this case the same order of cross-examination should operate, it is suggested, so that the child's lawyer comes last.

(2) Before the implementation of the Children and Young Persons (Amendment) Act 1986 (CYP(A)A), the next step in the

proceedings was to hear the respondent's case. But matters are complicated now that a parent or grandparent can be made a party to proceedings under ss. 32A or 32C of the CYPA 1969. In order that the respondent child's lawyer can fully evaluate the competing evidence and decide upon his approach to the court, it is suggested that these other parties should present their evidence and address the court at this stage, i.e. at the conclusion of the applicant's case.

(3) The practice whereby the child's or parent's lawyer makes a submission of no case to answer at the conclusion of the applicant's case has been condemned by the Divisional Court as inappropriate to care proceedings, since decisions in care cases should be made on the fullest of information, *M* v *Westminster CC* [1985] FLR 325.

(4) After the applicant and any other party have concluded their cases the child's lawyer presents his case. He can address the court either before or after calling his witnesses. Where witnesses are called they can be cross-examined by the applicant's lawyer and any other party to the proceedings. The rules are silent as to the order of cross-examination. If the parent is not a party, he can cross-examine, but again he is restricted to meeting allegations against him. The guardian ad litem can be called as a witness at this stage. After the evidence has been heard, the child's lawyer can address the court if he has not already done so when opening his case.

(5) The applicant can then bring evidence in rebuttal.

(6) The guardian ad litem has the opportunity at this stage to give evidence relevant to the applicant's case, whether or not he has already been called as a witness, r. 21 (3).

(7) If he has not already been allowed to do so the non-party parent or guardian can now recall and cross-examine any witness or call or give fresh evidence for the sole purpose of dealing with any allegations which have been made against him earlier in the proceedings.

(8) Any foster-parent or other person with whom the child has had his home for a period of not less than 42 days, ending not more than six months before the date of the application, must be notified of the date, time and place of the hearing, r. 14 (3) (*d*). A person notified under this rule has at this stage the limited right to make representations to the court. He may be legally represented. This rule recognizes that foster-parents and others, for example aunts and uncles, who have given a home to the child, can make a valuable contribution to the court's understanding of the child's welfare (see chapter 7).

Rule 19 goes further and permits representations from any person who can satisfy the court that he has demonstrated an interest in the child's welfare and that his representations are likely to be relevant to the proceedings and to the child's welfare (r. 19 (3) (*a*) and (*b*)).

(9) Finally both the child's and the applicant's lawyers can seek the leave of the court to address it a second time. Leave cannot be granted to one and not the other. If both apply for and obtain leave, the child's lawyer speaks first. The applicant's lawyer has the final word.

It must be stressed that the foregoing procedure is subject to the court's inherent jurisdiction to control its own proceedings and that frequently strict adherence to the procedure will not be appropriate.

4.6 Presentation of Reports

Where the court is satisfied that the applicant's case has been proved it must receive reports, r. 25 (3). At this stage it will receive and consider the report prepared by the guardian ad litem. The local authority have a duty to investigate the child's home surroundings, school record, health and character for the information of the court, CYPA 1969, s. 9 (1), and to provide further information on the above matters if requested to do so, s. 9 (2). They will almost always present this information in the form of a written report. At this stage any other written report of a probation officer, local authority, local education authority or medical practitioner may be received.

Such reports (so far as is practicable) must be made available to the parties, parents and child before the hearing, r. 25 (1). However, the court may direct that a report should not be disclosed to the child where this appears impracticable having regard to his age and understanding, or where it appears undesirable to do so having regard to serious harm which might thereby be suffered by him, r. 25 (1) (*f*). Where such a direction has been made, or where the child or his parent has been asked to withdraw from the court during the presentation of a report (r. 25 (3) (*e*)), the child 'shall be told the substance of any part of the information given to the court bearing on his character or conduct which the court considers to be material to the manner in which the case should be dealt with unless it appears to it impracticable so to do having regard to his age and understanding', r. 25 (4) (*a*). Similarly the parent, if present, 'shall be told the substance of any part of such information which the court considers to be material as aforesaid and which has reference to his character or conduct or to the character, conduct, home surroundings or health' of the child, r. 25 (4) (*b*). In either case, if the child or the parent wishes to produce further evidence relating to the substance of the report, and if the court thinks the further evidence would be material, it must adjourn the case. If necessary it must require the attendance at the adjourned hearing of the person who made the report. If adjournment is refused judicial review may be available, see *R v West Malling Juvenile Court ex parte K* [1986] 2 FLR 405. In that case a father was given copies of the social services' and guardian ad litem's reports on the morning of a hearing which turned out to be long and fiercely contested. The reports contained specific allegations against the father. He sought an adjournment in order to call witnesses in rebuttal but was refused. In granting judicial review the High Court held that the father had not had a fair hearing since he had not received a sufficiently detailed notice of the case. The local authority could have sent him a letter listing the heads of complaint or even have disclosed their witnesses' statements. But 'it is not enough to say that the facts were within the knowledge of this father. He is entitled to know the way in which the case is being put against him with sufficient particularity for him and his advisers to prepare his answer' (Wood J).

In practice, when all parties and parents agree, many juvenile courts conflate the proof and reports stages of care proceedings. Indeed, the magistrates may read all reports before hearing any evidence. While this approach is both sensible and supportable in an agreed case, it is suggested that it is unacceptable if objection is made, or where the application is opposed. Reports should be concerned with the disposition of the case, not its proof. The information contained in reports may, quite properly, be based on hearsay. This hearsay information may, correctly, be taken into account when the court is deciding what order it ought to make. But it would be wrong for hearsay evidence, which is generally inadmissible at the proof stage (see §1.3.6), to influence the court on its findings of fact. Accordingly, we would respectfully suggest that the judgment of Sheldon J in *Croydon LBC v N* [1987] 2 FLR 61 must be treated with great caution and perhaps be limited to the rather unusual circumstances of the case. For he says (obiter) that either the guardian ad litem's report or the social inquiry report, if otherwise unimpeachable and if its contents are relevant to the matter under consideration, can be produced in evidence and considered as such at any stage of the proceedings, and that r. 25 (3) does not preclude the earlier reception of the guardian ad litem's report in evidence if relevant and appropriate and proferred as such by the guardian.

4.7 Explanation of the Proposed Order

Before the court finally disposes of the case it must in simple language inform the child, his lawyer and his parent of the manner in which it proposes to deal with the case, and allow any of them to make representations, r. 27 (1). The applicant, however, does not have this further opportunity of addressing the court. On making the order the court has a duty to explain to the child in simple language its general nature and effect, unless this is impracticable having regard to the child's age and understanding. If the order requires the child's parent to enter into a recognizance, the court need not explain this to the child where it appears undesirable to do so, r. 27 (2).

4.8 Orders That May be Made

The court can make any of the following orders in respect of the child, CYPA 1969, s. 1 (3):

(a) an order requiring his parent or guardian to enter into a recognizance to take proper care of him and exercise proper control over him; or
(b) a supervision order; or
(c) a care order; or
(d) a hospital order within the meaning of Part III of the Mental Health Act 1983; or
(e) a guardianship order within the meaning of that Act; or
(f) if the offence condition is proved, an order of compensation to be paid to the victim or, in the case of a young person, a recognizance order for good behaviour, s. 3 (6), (7).

4.8.1 Hospital and guardianship orders

These orders can be made in respect of a child who is mentally ill. A hospital order authorizes the child's admission to and detention in a named hospital. A guardianship order places the child under the guardianship of a social services' department or any other person of whom the department approves. Both types of order must satisfy the conditions set out in s. 37 of the Mental Health Act 1983.

4.8.2 Recognizance order

A recognizance order requires the parent to enter into a recognizance (maximum amount of £1,000) to take proper care and to exercise proper control over the child, for a maximum period of three years, or until the child reaches eighteen. The order can be made only with the parent's consent, and if the parent fails to keep his promise he is liable to forfeit the whole or part of the sum specified in accordance with s. 120 of the Magistrates' Courts Act 1980. A recognizance order is not normally regarded as an appropriate response to care proceedings. It may occasionally be useful as a means of coercing a parent into the proper supervision of his child where proceedings are brought on the ground that the child is of compulsory school age and is not receiving efficient full-time education, CYPA 1969, s. 1 (2) (*e*).

4.8.3 Supervision order

A supervision order places a child under the supervision of the local authority in which area the child lives, or any other local authority which agree to supervise him. A child may be supervised by a probation officer where this is requested by the local authority and where the officer is already involved in the child's household, CYPA 1969, s. 13 (2).

The court can specify certain requirements. It can order that the child should reside with a named individual, provided that that person agrees, s. 12 (1). This is a significant provision; it could, for example, be used in a case where a foster-parent or relative has made representations to the court in the proceedings, or has been called as a witness. However, the legal status of the named individual is unclear (see §7.5.6). The court can include a requirement that the child should comply with directions given by the supervisor to live at a specified place, to present himself to a specified person and to participate in specified activities, s. 12 (2). These directions enable the supervisor to order intermediate treatment for the child, and it may be considered appropriate where the child is beyond control or not going to school.

A court can also include a requirement that the child shall be medically examined, s. 18 (2) (*b*). This may afford additional protection for a child considered to be at risk of neglect or ill-treatment. For example, the supervisor can arrange for the child to be periodically examined by his general practitioner or at a hospital. If this requirement or a requirement that the supervisor shall visit the child is not observed, s. 14A of the CYPA 1969 provides that a warrant to search for the child can be issued under s. 40 of the CYPA 1933 (see §3.3.2). More generally, if the parent refuses to take the child to a doctor or to permit him to be medically examined, the supervisor should consider whether the circumstances justify the making of a place of safety order under the CYPA 1969, s. 28, or whether an application should be made under s. 15 for the supervision order to be discharged with the recommendation that the court should substitute a care order. In such circumstances the court can substitute a care order without it being necessary to re-establish the primary ground.

A supervision order lasts for a maximum period of three years and ends on the child's eighteenth birthday. During the period of supervision the supervisor is under a general duty to advise, assist and befriend the child, CYPA 1969, s. 14.

4.8.4 Care order

A care order commits the child to the care of the local authority. The local authority have the same powers and duties over a child in care under a care order as a parent would have if no order had been made, Child Care Act 1980, s. 10 (2). However, the local authority have no right to change the child's religion, s. 10 (3); and they cannot agree to the child's adoption, or to an application to free the child for adoption. They can restrict access to the child, but where access by a parent is refused or terminated the parent can apply to a juvenile court for an access order (see chapter 5).

4.9 Discharge of Care Orders

A care order remains in force until the child is eighteen, unless the child was sixteen or over when the order was made, in which case it continues until he is nineteen, CYPA 1969, s. 20 (3) (*a*) and (*b*). An application to discharge a care order can be made by the local authority, the child, or his parent or guardian on his behalf, s. 21 (2) and s. 70 (2).

If the application is unopposed then the court *must* make a separate representation order unless satisfied that to do so is not necessary for safeguarding the interests of the child, s. 32A (2). In all other cases where before, or in the course of, the proceedings it appears to the court that there is or may be a conflict between the interests of the child and those of his parents, the court *may* order separate representation of the child, s. 32A (1). If a separate representation order is made, the court should appoint a guardian ad litem for the child, in an unopposed case 'unless satisfied that to do so is not necessary for safeguarding the interests of the child', s. 32B (1); in an opposed case 'if it appears to the court that it is in his interests to do so', CYP Rules 1988, r. 16 (1). The parent now becomes a party (see §4.2) and can apply to discharge the order in his own right.

4.9.1 Criteria for discharge

No specific criteria are laid down for the discharge of a care order. Section 21 (2) of the CYPA 1969 simply provides that the court may discharge the order if it appears that it is 'appropriate' to do so. Section 21 (2A) further provides that the court shall not discharge a care order where the child appears to be in need of care or control unless the court is satisfied that, whether through the making of a supervision order or otherwise, he will receive that care or control. In exercising its discretion the court is directed by the general principle that it must have regard to the welfare of the child, CYPA 1933, s. 44 (1). This test does not make the welfare of the child the first and paramount consideration. It has been variously stated (Cretney, *Principles of Family Law* 4th edn, pp. 542–3; Adcock and White [1980] JSWL 258) that juvenile courts tend to concentrate on whether the parent is fit and able to provide proper care and control, rather than on the needs of the child, and that 'unwrapping the language, what that really means is that [the applicants] have to show that there is no risk of the child being ill-treated if returned', *Re W* (1981) 2 FLR 360, at p. 367, per Ormrod LJ. However, s. 21 (2) does not compel the magistrates to discharge a care order if the primary condition(s) under which it was made no longer exist, see *R v Chertsey Justices ex parte E* [1987] 2 FLR 415 where it was held that the section gives the magistrates a discretion to decide whether discharge is in the interests of the child.

There is nevertheless a real risk that the child's interests may be overlooked where the evidence is mainly concentrated on the parent's current fitness to care. In almost all cases the child's interests will be better protected if a separate representation order is made, and if a guardian ad litem is appointed. The duty of the guardian ad litem is to give first and paramount consideration to the child's interests, and to make sure that the child's wishes and feelings are made known to the court. It is salutary to recall that the guardian ad litem provisions were introduced to prevent a repetition of the Maria Colwell tragedy, and to ensure that a child's views on the discharge application are fully made known to the court.

4.9.2 Orders on discharge

The court may simply discharge the care order, or it may discharge the order and substitute a supervision order, CYPA 1969, s. 21 (2). It must not discharge the care order or substitute a supervision order unless it is satisfied that through making a supervision order or otherwise, the child will receive the care or control he needs. The court has no power on a discharge application to make any other orders, such as an increase in access, a trial period at home, or a phased return (for the availability of wardship in this context, see §6.3.1).

4.10 Appeals

The child has a right of appeal against the making of an order, or the refusal to discharge an order, to the Crown Court, CYPA 1969, ss. 2 (12) and 21 (4). The appeal takes the form of a rehearing before a judge and two magistrates. The parent is entitled to exercise the right of appeal on behalf of the child, CYPA 1969, s. 21 (4), and where the court has made an order under s. 32A (1) of the Act disqualifying the parent from representing his child, the parent is entitled to appeal in his own right, CYPA 1969, ss. 2 (12), 21 (4A). Where an order has been made under s. 32A (1) but no guardian ad litem has been appointed, it is the duty of the solicitor acting for the child to consider whether notice of appeal should be served, *R v Plymouth Juvenile Court ex parte F and F* [1987] 1 FLR 169. Legal aid is obtainable and the Crown Court has power to appoint a guardian ad litem, Crown Court Rules 1982, r. 9 (2).

It should be noted that neither the local authority nor the guardian ad litem can appeal against either the court's refusal to make an order or its discharge of an existing order. If the local authority believe that the juvenile court's decision puts the child at risk they may invoke the wardship jurisdiction, or permit the guardian ad litem to do so, *Re D (A Minor) (Justices' Decision: Review)* [1977] Fam. 158; *Re C (A Minor)* (1981) 2 FLR 62; and they can do this even where a parent has made a successful appeal on behalf of the child to the Crown Court, *Hertfordshire CC v Dolling* (1982) 3 FLR 423 (see §6.3.1). Where an appeal is on a point of law only, it proceeds by way of case stated to the Family Division.

5 ACCESS TO CHILDREN IN CARE

5.1 Introduction

Section 18 of the Child Care Act 1980 (CCA) requires a local authority to give first consideration to the welfare of each child in their care. Occasionally this duty necessitates a decision to refuse, terminate or reduce a parent's access to a child. The decision may well be part of a specific plan for the child, such as placement for adoption or with long-term foster-parents. Until January 1984 local authorities enjoyed complete autonomy over access to those children for whom they exercised parental rights. An unsuccessful attempt to challenge an access decision was made in wardship proceedings in *Re W (Minors) (Wardship: Jurisdiction)* [1980] Fam. 60, and in 1981 the House of Lords confirmed that a local authority had a largely unreviewable discretion in the matter, see *A* v *Liverpool CC* (1981) 2 FLR 222. Allegations that some local authorities were behaving in a high-handed fashion, and the general feeling that natural parents should be able to challenge a decision to deny them access, led to Sch. I of the Health and Social Services and Social Security Adjudications Act 1983, which inserted Part IA (ss. 12A–12G) into the CCA 1980. This is supported by a Code of Practice prepared by the DHSS for the guidance of local authorities (hereinafter referred to as the Code).

Briefly, a parent, guardian or custodian who is refused access or whose access is terminated has the right to apply to a juvenile court for an access order requiring the local authority to arrange access. Part IA of the Act sets out the framework whereby qualified parties can challenge local authority decisions on access in the juvenile court.

5.1.1 Children covered

It is important to note that s. 12A (1) of the CCA 1980 applies the following access provisions to a wide range of children who have been taken into care by a variety of statutory routes. The provisions also apply to children in the care of voluntary organizations in which parental rights and duties have been vested, CCA 1980, s. 64 (8). They do *not* apply to the following:

(1) Children in voluntary care by virtue of s. 2 of the CCA 1980 (see chapter 2). The omission is understandable, firstly since the parent can demand the return of his child and the local authority then have no authority to retain it, and secondly since s. 2 (3) obliges the authority to try, if possible, to return the child to its family. In this situation termination or refusal of access is clearly an inappropriate response.

(2) Children subject to a place of safety order under s. 28 of the Children and Young Persons Act 1969.

(3) Children committed to care by the High Court, CCA 1980, s. 12A (2); or by the High or county court after divorce and related proceedings, because these courts already have the power to insert directions as to access in these cases, Matrimonial Causes Act 1973, s. 43 (5) (*a*), and see *Re R (A Minor) (Child in Care: Access)* (1983) 4 FLR 787.

5.2 Who Can Apply?

Part IA is available to a natural parent, but not the father of an illegitimate child, CCA 1980, s. 87 (1) and see *Re TD (A Minor) (Wardship: Jurisdiction)* [1985] FLR 1150; *Re M and H (Minors)* [1988] 3 WLR 485; to a guardian, that is a person appointed as such by deed or will or by order of a court, s. 87 (1); or to a custodian. 'Custodian' is defined as a person given legal custody of a child under a custodianship order, CYP Rules 1988, r. 29 (2). This narrow interpretation means that neither a person with actual custody nor a person given legal custody by a court order such as a step-parent who is given custody by a divorce court, can apply under Part IA. This wider concept of custody is expressly included in Part I of the Act by s. 8 (2), but has no counterpart in Part IA.

It is clear that, in the absence of a court order of guardianship or custodianship, the child's wider family cannot take advantage of Part IA, although the Code (para. 8) instructs the local authority to take into account the child's wider family, such as siblings and grandparents. It should also be noted that the child cannot apply for an access order under these provisions. For the position of the father of an illegitimate child, see §7.6.

5.3 Meaning of Access

Access is not defined in the statute. It can be used either to facilitate the reunification of a family or to maintain contact between the parties where the child is likely to suffer by the termination of access. It means direct personal contact between child and parents and varies from visits by the parents to the local authority's premises, with or without third party supervision during the access, to staying access whereby the child is allowed to stay in the parental home for weekends or school holidays. As to the process of access, the Code is silent and much will depend upon the overall policy of each local authority towards the usefulness of access. This will then be translated into guidance issued to social workers. Knowledge of these internal instructions leads lawyers not only to a better understanding of the causes of access disputes but also to a better assessment of the merits of a local authority's conduct. However, for the private practitioner access to this guidance depends upon the benevolence of the local authority. For local authorities, some helpful advice can be gleaned from the Code, for example, paras. 17, 21, 25 and 26, and also from the commonsense suggestions in the Visiting Code proposed by Justice in its Report on Parental Rights and Duties (1975) which makes the obvious, but important, point that the access arrangements should not be rigidly regular to the annoyance of the child or to the inconvenience of the parent. It may be useful for a local authority to acquaint their officers, and in particular foster-parents, with the Visiting Code and even to use it as a basis for devising their own code of practice.

In the absence of a definition it can be argued that 'access' should be interpreted broadly so as to include contact by correspondence and telephone, particularly when correspondence can be seen by the parent as an important precursor to visiting access or as an alternative way of maintaining some contact with an older child. If this is accepted, a court could deny visits yet order access by correspondence or telephone. The traditional approach, however, does not regard access so widely, in which case the local authority retain complete discretion over the method of access. The only way in which the court could interfere would be by attaching conditions to an access order as to correspondence or telephone calls, though this would require a generous interpretation of the power to attach conditions contained in the CCA 1980, s. 12C (3).

5.4 Background to Access Disputes

Statute has little guidance for local authorities as to how access should be determined. They are bound to place the child's welfare as the first consideration in planning his future, CCA 1980, s. 18. In addition s. 21 (1) directs that the child should be placed near his home, but only where this is consistent with his welfare. From the parents' point of view, the location of their child's placement may be crucial to their maintaining regular access. As far as the Code is concerned, it offers guidance on all aspects of access. For example, it highlights the need for speed in reaching a decision (para. 7), the wisdom of listening to the child's views (para. 11) and of considering access to the wider family (para. 8) and the benefits of regular communication with parents (para. 15). Many local authorities have implemented the Code's recommendation to produce explanatory leaflets (para. 16).

There is a presumption running through the Code that access to his natural parents will normally benefit the child. Consequently reunification of the family will be the first and most common goal for the authority to seek. But, as will be seen (§5.5), when a dispute over access reaches litigation, the sole test for the juvenile court is the child's best interests. Social workers should be aware of this statutory criterion for it may encourage them to deny access more readily at an early stage. The Code (paras. 28, 29) also requires local authorities to set up a machinery to hear grievances from parents so that the social worker's decision on access can be reviewed by senior officers. This procedure can be a very useful mechanism for resolving misconceptions and disputes between the parties at an early stage and for avoiding formal legal proceedings. It is especially important for the parent since he can raise a variety of complaints over access, for example, that access arrangements are inconvenient or that it has been unfairly reduced, whereas, as will be seen (§5.5), his right to invoke the jurisdiction of the juvenile court is limited to complaints about the local authority's refusal or termination of access.

5.4.1. Status of the Code

For the most part the Code is a short collection of commonsense guidelines. What status does it enjoy? If a local authority ignore one of the Code's more specific enjoinders, for example, by failing to confirm a decision in writing (para. 15) or by improperly using access arrangements as a method of controlling a child (para. 24) or by failing to inform the parents in advance that termination of access is under consideration (para. 33), has the parent any legal redress?

Two separate but related matters need to be considered. First, is a local authority legally obliged to obey the Code? The Act is silent as to the Code's effect. It could possibly be regarded as 'general guidance of the Secretary of State' under the Local Authority Social Services

Act 1970, s. 7 (1), in which case a local authority must observe it. But this approach does not mean that failure to observe it entitles a third party to legal redress. If that had been intended, Parliament in the statute or the Secretary of State in the foreword to the Code, could specifically and easily have so provided. Moreover, the general nature of many of the Code's provisions does not easily accord with the imposition of precise legal duties which statutes and statutory instruments customarily generate.

It may be asked, secondly, to what extent the Code can be used to interpret the statute. The courts' initial reaction has varied. In *M v Berkshire CC* [1985] FLR 257 the Court of Appeal referred to the Code 'as an aid to construction' of the statute. In contrast, in *R v Bolton MBC ex parte B* [1985] FLR 343, the Divisional Court refused to use the Code 'as a guide to the proper meaning of the words of the statutes'. Instead, having reached an interpretation of the statutory words in s. 12B (4) and (5), the court held that it could then look to see if that interpretation conflicted with the Code.

It is suggested, first, that breach of the Code alone will not give parents and other persons a right of redress against a local authority. But, secondly, a breach of the Code's more important provisions may be valuable evidence to support an action for judicial review on the basis that an authority have acted improperly and therefore beyond their statutory powers. For example, if a local authority severely reduce access but do not terminate it, review of their decision may still be possible (see §5.5.1), and evidence that they have made access infrequent and physically inconvenient in breach of the Code (paras. 5, 10, 25 and 26) would be strong support for such a review. (For the potential scope of judicial review, see §6.5.) Thirdly, if, at the hearing for an access order, the parent's advocate is able to establish a breach of a major provision in the Code, the court may well be influenced so as to grant an access order on the merits. In contrast, breach of a minor requirement will risk a word of censure from the court at most. Finally, if it proved possible to mount any civil action against a local authority for the way in which they have treated a child, cf. *Gaskin* v *Liverpool CC* [1980] 1 WLR 1549, infringement of the Code could be valuable evidence.

5.5 Termination or Refusal of Access

Before a local authority (or voluntary organization exercising parental rights) terminate or refuse access to a parent, guardian or custodian (but not other persons, for example, grandparents), they must tell them in writing that this action is being considered, what its implications will be, how they can voice their views and how the final decision will be conveyed to them, Code, para. 33. This advance warning can give parents the opportunity to seek legal advice and prepare for action. They could, for example, acquaint themselves with the Code and see if its provisions have been observed, or they could seek a discussion of the case with senior management in the social services department. However, very little time may intervene between the warning and the next step, which is written notification of the authority's decision, in the form prescribed by the Access (Notice of Termination and of Refusal) Order, SI 1983 No. 1860. Access ends on service of this notice.

5.5.1 Termination

If a local authority are considering whether to terminate existing access, they must reach a decision urgently. Indeed it has been decided in *R* v *Bolton MBC ex parte B* [1985] FLR 343 that 14 days and exceptionally 21 are sufficient for an authority to make up their mind. Similarly, once a decision to terminate has been reached, the parent must be informed of it and served with notice without delay. This means, for example, that a local authority cannot end access informally and tell the parent that they 'will reach a final decision in due course' or 'will review the decision in a month's time'.

It is specifically provided that a local authority are not to be taken to terminate access in a case where they propose to substitute new arrangements for access for existing arrangements, s. 12B (4). An authority thus retain a considerable discretion to vary access. But what is the position if the authority decide that rehabilitation of the child with the parents is impracticable and they therefore reduce access drastically to, for example, one hour three times a year? In *Re Y (Minors)* [1988] 1 FLR 299 it was argued that such limited arrangements cannot properly be called 'access' and that access had in reality been terminated. This argument failed, Bush J holding that it is impossible to draw the line at which access becomes so minimal that it amounts to a termination or refusal. If the court were to draw such a line, it would be encroaching upon territory that Parliament has expressly put at the discretion of local authorities.

However, it was also stated in *Re Y (Minors)* that if it were possible to prove that a particular local authority had kept access alive on a minimum basis, solely for the purpose of preventing an application for access being made to a juvenile court, then an application could be made for judicial review under RSC Ord. 53; see too the *obiter* remarks in *M* v *Berkshire CC* [1985] FLR 257. This would require clear evidence that the authority had acted wrongly, for example, through malice, or in such a way that no reasonable authority could have acted thus. Inevitably there will be an element of uncertainty as to whether one visit three times a year is merely token and intended to thwart a parent's right to litigate the matter, or whether the authority have genuinely decided that rehabilitation of child and parent is impracticable but that some small contact should be maintained. Clearly, the burden lies on the aggrieved parent to establish an abuse of power and, since the authority retain a wide discretion over the frequency of access, their decision is generally unreviewable on the ground of unreasonableness. Furthermore, the fact that a court or another authority might have exercised that discretion differently will not suffice, *Re Y (Minors)* (and see §6.5).

5.5.2 Refusal

Termination consists of the ending of pre-existing access arrangements, whereas refusal covers the situation where no access has yet been afforded, *R v Bolton MBC ex parte B* [1985] FLR 343. Clearly the parent should make a specific request for access before it can be 'refused', preferably in writing or by his solicitor. If made orally, a careful note of the conversation should be kept. It is provided that a local authority are not to be taken to refuse to make arrangements for access in a case where they postpone access for such reasonable period as appears to them to be necessary to enable them to consider what arrangements for access (if any) are to be made, s. 12B (5). In *R v Bolton MBC* (above), it was stated that termination of access could be postponed for 14 or at most 21 days. This suggests that *refusal* of access could take longer. Indeed a local authority may need to undertake lengthier investigations into the desirability of access where the child is newly received into care. As Wood J observed:

'. . . a substantial time – certainly weeks and possibly months – may be required before making a decision in the initial stages of care, for example it may be necessary to take psychiatric advice when dealing with a child seriously disturbed as a result of emotional or physical trauma, yet the longer the history of care, together with its evidence of success or failure of access, the easier and quicker should it be possible to reach a decision whether or not to continue or revive access.'

However, as *R v Bolton MBC* (above) and the Code (para. 7) make clear, the local authority's thinking time is limited. The authority cannot delay their decision for an unreasonable time or for ulterior motives, for example, because adoption or custodianship proceedings

are pending and they feel that the issue of access can be more fully
dealt with in those proceedings (see §5.7).

5.6 Action Open to the Parent

The notice of termination or refusal served on the parent will tell
him of his right to apply to a juvenile court to contest the decision
and advise him to seek legal advice. The parent must act by way of
complaint, s. 12C (2), and the complaint must be made within six
months of receipt of the notice, Magistrates' Courts Act 1980, s. 127.
This can lead to uncertainty for the child and local authority if the
parent leaves it until the last minute before acting. It could also lead
to injustice if, for whatever reason, the parent applies too late and
loses his right to object. It has been stated in *Y* v *Kirklees MC* [1985]
FLR 927 that in the latter situation it is open to the parent to make
a fresh application to the local authority for access. The authority
must consider it and on refusal must serve a fresh notice on the
parent. A new six months' time limit for complaint would then run.
It will be appreciated, however, that time will count against the
parents on the merits of the case and, unless good reason is
established, a much delayed application for an access order will
reduce the chances of success. Parents and their advisers should
therefore move swiftly. It also behoves the courts to avoid unnecessary
adjournments, especially when access is refused at the outset. For,
as the Code acknowledges (para. 6), the first weeks in care are likely
to be particularly crucial to the success of the relationship between
the parent, the social worker and the child's carers and to the level
of future contact between parent and child. It is at this time that
patterns are set which it may be difficult to change.

  If the local authority fail to serve the proper statutory notice of
their decision or reach their decision unlawfully (cf. the facts of *R* v
Bolton MBC ex parte B [1985] FLR 343, where the authority decided
to postpone notification in preference to adoption proceedings),
judicial review would be open to the parent. If, on the other hand,
they breach the Code, for example, by failing to consult the Director
of Social Services (para. 32) a parent's redress will depend upon the
legal status of the Code (see §5.4.1).

5.7 The Hearing

Whether the Act is used regularly will depend greatly on the policy
of each local authority towards parental access and whether they

favour adoption. The most difficult cases facing a juvenile court will be those where the local authority have decided on adoption and have terminated access and the parent then applies for an access order. In the meantime the local authority may have embarked on freeing for adoption proceedings under s. 18 of the Adoption Act 1976.

It has been suggested in *R* v *Slough Justices ex parte B* [1985] FLR 384 that once the authority decide on adoption they should act with great speed. The authority could therefore apply for a freeing for adoption order at an early stage, even when no adopters have been selected or even simultaneously with, or just prior to, their decision on access. An unseemly rush for the courts may result – the local authority in the magistrates' court, county court or High Court asking for a freeing order and the parents in the juvenile court asking for access. Where magistrates take the view that it would not be right to proceed because the issue of access is so bound up with the issue of adoption, they can adjourn the proceedings pending the decision on adoption, *R* v *Slough Justices ex parte B* (above); *C* v *Berkshire CC* [1987] 2 FLR 210. However, it has also been held that it is highly desirable for the access proceedings to be heard first in the juvenile court and that the adoption proceedings should be stayed, *Southwark LB* v *H* [1985] FLR 989. The position would seem to be that the magistrates can properly adjourn the access proceedings where they are satisfied that the adoption proceedings are advancing expeditiously. But the power of adjournment is not to be exercised automatically, and certainly not in cases where the adoption proceedings are likely to be delayed.

The course suggested in the *Southwark* case reduces the multiplicity of proceedings but also highlights the fact that the access hearing is far from a mere formality. For if an access order is refused, success in adoption will be virtually assured. If an access order is made, the local authority's plans will be turned upside down. In this event, one solution is for the authority to appeal to the High Court, CCA 1980, s. 12C (5). In the meantime the adoption application could be lodged in the High Court, which would then be seized of both sets of proceedings, and consolidation could follow, see RSC Ord. 4, r. 9 (see too §6.3.3).

The importance of the access proceedings will usually require a very full hearing of the evidence. A particular problem sometimes facing the authority's lawyer will be the threat to the anonymity of the adopters which access proceedings pose. Their evidence may be crucial to the local authority's case, yet the court's power to hear evidence in the absence of a parent does not extend to this situation, CYP Rules 1988, r. 35.

5.7.1 The child's welfare

In contrast to the rest of child-care law and indeed to the rest of the CCA 1980, the child's welfare is the first and paramount consideration for the juvenile court in an access hearing, s. 12F (1). This will generally work to the benefit of the local authority. Of the many relevant factors, much can depend on how long the child has been with foster-parents and whether they are being considered as potential adopters; and similarly whether the natural parents can realistically expect to be given care of the child in the near future (time being of the essence for the child). Hence the local authority's lawyer should urge the court to look closely at what home and opportunities the parents can offer. Also if the purpose of the application is merely to retain limited access, without long-term reunification of the family, the application can be regarded as futile and as seriously disruptive to the child, see *Devon CC* v *C* [1985] FLR 619; *Re M* [1988] 1 FLR 35. Indeed, it would usually be wrong for a juvenile court to 'test the water' by ordering an experimental period of access in such a case. The child may have been prepared for adoption and it can be powerfully argued that access by a parent is certain to unsettle him and is not in his best interests.

It has been clearly stated in the Court of Appeal that an application to a juvenile court for access can be made under Part IA of the CCA 1980 even though a care order has only recently been made and even though the local authority regard rehabilitation of child and parent as impracticable (Slade LJ in *M* v *Berkshire CC* [1985] FLR 257). In reality, however, the local authority will frequently hold the upper hand, and a juvenile court may well be strongly influenced by the fact of a recent, unappealed care order and the local authority's plans for the child. Although the Code suggests a presumption in favour of access, Sir John Arnold P has issued a sharp reminder of the correct position:

'The function of a court trying a contested access application must always be to put the interests of the child first and to consider whether, in the particular circumstances of the case, it is favourable from the child's point of view that there should be an order for access, and only if that is the case should the court come to a conclusion in favour of access. This is not a matter which should be influenced by the conception that the natural parent has a right to that access to the child. That right is a right which is the product of the court's decision, and that decision should only be made if it is demonstrated that the access asked for is favourable to the child and, in order to come to a conclusion upon that matter, the court is bound to pay regard, and substantial regard, in the balancing exercise to those factors which are relevantly put forward as factors militating against the conclusion that, in the particular case, access to the child is a desirable development in the interests of the child.' *Hereford and Worcester CC* v *JAH* [1985] FLR 530.

This important observation deserves emphasis: access should not be given too readily, but only if it is to the child's advantage. So even if the court finds that the parents have deep feelings for their child, these feelings are largely irrelevant unless access is going to be beneficial to the child, *Coventry CC* v *T* [1988] 2 FLR 301. Of particular importance will be the evidence of the guardian ad litem and of expert witnesses, such as a paediatrician, child psychiatrist, educational psychologist, and health visitor as to the likely effect of continued or renewed access on the child's development. The Court of Appeal has held, in the context of a custody and access dispute between parents, that where a child has been sexually abused any access arrangements requiring strict supervision are unlikely to be beneficial to the child, and that access to the child by the abuser should be refused, *Re R (A Minor)* [1988] 1 FLR 206; *S* v *S* [1988] 1 FLR 213.

5.7.2 Making the child a party

In some cases there is a possibility that the child's point of view will go by default. For example, the parties (the local authority and parents) may be so violently opposed that there is a danger that the child's interests will not be adequately represented to the court. The court may make the child a party to the proceedings where it considers it necessary in order to safeguard the interests of the child, s. 12F (2). The initiative will usually come from the court and justices should always be alert to the possibility. There will, however, be cases where the parties' representatives identify the difficulty. In this case, as officers of the court, they should suggest the action. Unless satisfied that it is unnecessary, the court should then appoint a guardian ad litem to safeguard the child's interests, s. 12F (3). He in turn must act according to a list of duties set out in the CYP Rules 1988, r. 31 (6). There is no guidance as to when a child should be made a party to proceedings and a guardian ad litem appointed. Ideally these powers should be exercised early in the proceedings and a single justice or, more commonly, the justices' clerk will act. Yet the amount of evidence available to him may be slender. It is suggested that he should always err on the side of exercising these powers.

It should be noted that there is no statutory obligation for the child to be brought before the court, and it has been held that it is not in the interests of the child, the court or the parent for the child physically to be produced, *A* v *Wigan MBC* [1986] 1 FLR 608.

5.8 The Order

The court's order will require the local authority to allow a parent, guardian or custodian to have access to the child. It will usually be sensible for the court to specify the type of access in some detail because of the probable ill-feeling or tension between the parties. This can easily create a dilemma for the court. On the one hand, rigid access provisions clearly prevent the flexibility which parties often need to adapt to changing circumstances and consequently a juvenile court will be well advised to try to build in flexibility by making an order for 'reasonable access'. On the other hand, such an order will often be inappropriate, since it leaves too much day-to-day control to the local authority, which by definition desires to terminate access, cf. *Devon CC* v *C* [1985] FLR 619. The juvenile court can in fact insert conditions into an access order as to its 'commencement, frequency, duration or place of access or to any other matter for which it appears to the court that provision ought to be made in connection with the requirement to allow access', s. 12C (3). It is suggested that this provision could not be stretched to permit access to the wider family. This would contradict the preceding words of s. 12C (3), which speak only of access to a parent, guardian or custodian. Nonetheless s. 12C (3) is potentially very wide. Consequently, the parties, and in particular the guardian ad litem if the child is a party, should during preparation of the case consider the possibility of asking the court to specify access, and should be ready to suggest to the court what those specifications should be.

5.9 Appeal

An appeal from the juvenile court lies to the Divisional Court of the Family Division within six weeks, RSC Ord. 90, r. 9. However, the courts are anxious to avoid delay in child cases and the President of the Family Division has agreed that the maximum acceptable delay before the hearing of an appeal is 28 days, *Hereford and Worcester CC* v *EH* [1985] FLR 975. It follows that a very good reason would be needed to justify a longer delay; delay generally can affect the court's assessment of the merits of the case; and a local authority should not allow delay to interfere with any plan, such as preparation for adoption, which they have for the child.

Any decision of a juvenile court including an interim order of a procedural nature amounts to a 'decision' for the purpose of s. 12C (5) and can therefore be appealed, *Southwark LBC* v *H* [1985] FLR 989. The right of appeal is statutory and the Family Division can hear appeals on both law and fact. Indeed *R* v *Slough Justices ex parte B* [1985] FLR 384 encouraged litigants to use the statutory right of appeal to hear questions of fact and of law. This approach ensures, unlike judicial review, that the merits of the case are dealt with on appeal. It can also be obtained quickly by appeal by notice of motion and by a request for an expedited hearing; see *Hereford and Worcester CC* v *EH* (above).

As to the scope of an appeal, in *Devon CC* v *C* [1985] FLR 619 it was said that the Family Division:

'. . . will not interfere with the justices' decisions unless they were plainly wrong or had been reached by some erroneous reasoning, or by their having taken or having omitted to take into account some consideration which they should have ignored or for which they should have had proper regard. It is not sufficient to justify any interference by this court merely that if it had been asked at first instance to conduct the first balancing exercise it would have reached a different conclusion.'

This is in line with the approach approved by the House of Lords in child custody cases, see *G* v *G (Minors: Custody Appeal)* [1985] FLR 894, and which gives the juvenile court a generous ambit of unreviewable discretion. On the other hand, where the justices have plainly erred, an appellate judge is fully justified in setting aside their decision and adjudicating himself on the merits, see *Re M (A Minor)* [1988] 1 FLR 35.

It should be noted that since the appeal is a rehearing, the court can receive fresh evidence and dispose of the case on that basis. The 'paramountcy' test of the child's welfare can be a very important factor in persuading the appellate court to admit fresh evidence, see *Devon CC* v *C* (above). It should be noted that an appeal from the juvenile court is open to the parents, to the guardian ad litem on behalf of the child, CYP Rules 1988, r. 31 (7), and, unlike in care proceedings, to the local authority. Finally, in some difficult cases wardship may be the appropriate alternative to the statutory framework for a local authority, see *Re LH (A Minor)* [1986] 2 FLR 306, the dicta in *Re M (A Minor)* (above) and §6.4.3.

5.10 Variation and Discharge

Either the person in whose favour an access order has been made or
the local authority may apply for its variation or discharge, s. 12D.
In some cases the local authority will have slender or marginal
grounds for appealing the initial access order and they will need to
monitor its operation for a period before applying for a variation or
discharge. In all cases it is open to the parent and local authority
informally to vary the terms of an access order to accommodate
changing circumstances. For example, if an access condition proves
to be unworkable or the parent considers the visits to be too
infrequent, there is no reason why the condition should not be
modified. However, there will come a time when it is prudent for
the party in whose favour the change has been made to seek its
official endorsement from the juvenile court.

5.11 Emergency Orders

If the local authority believe that an access order is detrimental to
the child, they can seek, *ex parte* if necessary, an emergency order
which lasts for up to seven days and which suspends the access order,
s. 12E. The authority must satisfy a single magistrate that continued
access 'will put the child's welfare seriously at risk'. This course of
action has the attraction that if, during the seven or fewer days, the
local authority apply for variation or termination of the order, the
suspension of access will last until the full hearing, s. 12E (3).
However, this is an emergency provision which is to be used only
where there is a serious risk to the child's welfare. In a less serious
case the authority should apply to vary or discharge the access order,
in which case the welfare of the child is the court's first and paramount
consideration.

6 WARDSHIP AND OTHER REMEDIES

6.1 Introduction

There are some occasions when, if all else fails in the statutory child-care framework, the practitioner should be alert to the possibilities of invoking the wardship jurisdiction of the High Court and, to a lesser extent, judicial review, habeas corpus, the Local Ombudsman or the European Convention for the Protection of Human Rights.

6.2 Wardship

Wardship is an ancient jurisdiction, originating in the royal prerogative and now exercised by the Family Division of the High Court. It is designed to protect and assist all children under the age of eighteen who are present in England and Wales, and children who are British citizens, wherever they are situated. Relevant aspects of the jurisdiction are found in the Family Law Reform Act 1969, s. 7, the procedures are set out in RSC Ord. 90 and various Practice Directions, and its scope is contained in an expanding body of jurisprudence. In the child-care field, wardship can have advantages over the child-care statutes, and, most importantly, it can safeguard the welfare of the child when other procedures and remedies are unavailable or have failed.

6.2.1. Procedure

An application for wardship is made by originating summons issued out of either the principal registry of the Family Division or a district registry. The mere making of an application means that the child becomes a ward, Supreme Court Act 1981, s. 41. However, if an appointment for the hearing of the summons is not obtained within 21 days, the child ceases to be a ward at the end of that period. An application for wardship can be made *ex parte*, but only where this is

89

a matter of urgent necessity, *Re H (A Minor) (Adoption)* [1985] FLR 519. In most cases it will be unnecessary to make the child a party, because his interests will be adequately represented in the welfare officer's report, see *Practice Direction (Child: Joinder as Party)* [1982] 1 WLR 118. But in special cases of difficulty, when the child is made a party, the Official Solicitor may become involved, and his expertise can be of particular benefit to advancing the child's interests. As to his appointment and the payment of his costs, see *Practice Direction (Child: Joinder as Party)* (above) (and §1.9).

6.3 When Wardship is Available to Local Authorities

Much of the contemporary importance of wardship derives from its use in coming to the assistance of local authorities. Such use was clearly approved by the House of Lords in *A* v *Liverpool CC* (1981) 2 FLR 222 and *W* v *Hertfordshire CC* [1985] FLR 879, and subsequently by the Court of Appeal in *Re R* [1987] 2 FLR 400. It has been variously described as a jurisdiction to supplement statutory powers or to fill gaps or lacunae in the law. It is undoubtedly correct that wardship can assist local authorities when their statutory powers of intervention are unavailable or have run their course. However, the jurisdiction appears to be more readily available than this, and local authorities appear to be entitled to call in aid the prerogative jurisdiction at will, whether or not the statutory jurisdiction has been exhausted or has failed to protect the child, *Re LH* [1986] 2 FLR 306; *Stockport MBC* v *B*; *Stockport MBC* v *L* [1986] 2 FLR 80; *Re M* [1988] 1 FLR 35.

While the statutory framework normally provides adequate protection for children at risk, there are some situations in which it fails. These are outlined below.

6.3.1 Care proceedings

When a local authority realize that they will be unable to satisfy the requirements of s. 1 of the Children and Young Persons Act 1969 (CYPA), they can invoke wardship. An example would be when fear is expressed about the future safety of a first-born child, still at the maternity hospital. Since s. 1 (2) (*a*) of the CYPA 1969 is couched in the present tense, and since the baby is hardly at risk in the hospital, the Act is unavailable (see §3.4.3) and thus the only way to protect the child is through making him a ward, cf. *Re C (A Minor)*

(Wardship: Surrogacy) [1985] FLR 846 *sub nom. Re A Baby.* Similarly, when a local authority fail to secure or retain a care order under the CYPA 1969, they do not have a right of appeal on the merits. In this situation it was held by Dunn J in *Re D (A Minor) (Justices' Decision: Review)* [1977] Fam. 158 that the statutory scheme can be regarded as stepping aside, and that far from local authorities being discouraged from applying to the court in wardship, they should be encouraged to do so. (See also *Hertfordshire CC v A* (1981) *The Times*, December 15 and *Re C (A Minor)* (1981) 2 FLR 62.) The Court of Appeal, in *Re R* [1987] 2 FLR 400, endorsed this approach to the wardship jurisdiction and emphasized that a local authority must be at liberty to invoke wardship if and when it is deemed necessary in the interests of the child. One such reason is that the welfare of the child is the 'golden thread' which guides the court in wardship, whereas in care proceedings statutory grounds for intervention must be established. In the case of a discharge application, the weight to be given to the welfare of the child is unclear and it may be that juvenile courts tend to concentrate on whether the child will come to harm if returned home rather than on wider considerations concerning the child's best interests (see §4.8.1).

Furthermore, the High Court has much wider powers than a juvenile court, which can only make, or refuse to make, care and supervision orders. (Its other powers arise in special circumstances deriving from the Mental Health Act 1983, see §4.6.1.) A judge of the High Court, by contrast, can make orders which are specifically adaptable to the situation which has arisen. For example, he can order access, place the child in the care of relatives or third parties or order that steps be taken to rehabilitate the child with his family (though there is a risk that such an order may be flouted, see *Re D (A Minor) (Wardship: Access)* [1987] 2 FLR 365). Most importantly a juvenile court cannot order that a child's return home should be phased, so wardship may be the only way to protect him from the abrupt effect of a successful discharge application (see *Hertfordshire CC v Dolling* (1982) 3 FLR 423).

6.3.2 Children in voluntary care

If a child has been in care on a voluntary basis under s. 2 of the CCA 1980 for less than six months and the parent demands his immediate return, it may be that a local authority cannot lawfully pass a s. 3 resolution assuming parental rights over him, see *Lewisham LBC v Lewisham Juvenile Court Justices* [1980] AC 273 (and §2.2.1). Consequently the authority have no right to keep the child in care, but, as Lord Salmon pointed out in that case, the authority may

seize, take over

consider it to be their 'moral duty' to seek wardship where they are concerned for the child's fate. This approach to wardship can also be supported on the basis that the statutory scheme no longer applies and that therefore wardship is not usurping the function of Parliament, but rather it is fulfilling its proper role of protecting children, cf. the reasoning in *Re S (An Infant)* [1965] 1 WLR 483 and *Re R(K) (An Infant)* [1964] Ch 455.

When a local authority fail in the juvenile court to obtain an order that a parental rights resolution should not lapse they have a right of appeal to the Family Division. But this has the disadvantage that the appellate court must adjudicate on the proper interpretation of s. 3 of the CCA 1980. Often this requires the local authority to prove that the parent has been culpable to a high degree, which is a difficult burden to discharge, see §2.3. Furthermore, when a child has been in care for some length of time, his best interests and his parents' culpability may turn on quite different considerations, such as the strength of his attachment to his foster-parents, despite access visits by his parents, cf. *W* v *Nottinghamshire CC* (1982) 3 FLR 33. Thus the more flexible approach of wardship may be preferable. Considerations of this nature led to wardship being invoked after parents had successfully appealed the juvenile court's decision in *Wheatley* v *London Borough of Waltham Forest* [1979] 2 WLR 543; *O'Dare Ai* v *South Glamorgan CC* (1982) 3 FLR 1; *Crosby (A Minor)* v *Northumberland CC* (1982) 12 Fam. Law 92.

6.3.3. Denial of access

Permanency planning, coupled with a desire to avoid a child 'drifting' in care, will often be the motivation behind a local authority's decision to refuse or terminate access by a parent. Sometimes adoption is selected as the best way of securing the child's long-term interests. However, implementation of these plans is liable to be frustrated if, after receipt of the formal notice of refusal or termination, the parent makes a successful application for access to a juvenile court (see §5.7). Instead of risking this it may be advisable for the local authority to ward the child at the outset and to seek leave from the judge either to place the child for adoption, or to apply for an order freeing him for adoption under s. 18 of the Adoption Act 1976, see *Re LH (A Minor)* [1986] 2 FLR 306; *Re M (A Minor)* [1988] 1 FLR 35, and cf. *Coventry CC* v *T* [1986] 2 FLR 301.

Where an access order has been made by a juvenile court a local authority have a right to appeal it under the CCA 1980, s. 6. However, it was stated in *Re LH (A Minor)* (above) that the existence of a statutory right of appeal does not preclude wardship. It is arguable that resort to wardship here is unjustifiable, for the paramountcy of the child's welfare applies identically in the juvenile court (CCA 1980, s. 12F (1)) and the juvenile court has wide powers to insert conditions into the order. Thus wardship is here being used to evade any restrictions normally obtaining on a court in the exercise of its appellate function in an access appeal, namely that the decision of the trial court must be shown to have been clearly wrong, *Devon CC v C* [1985] FLR 619; *G v G (Minors)* [1985] FLR 894 and see §5.9. It is not being used because the statutory scheme is too narrowly drafted to enable the authority properly to fulfil their protective function. In *A v Liverpool CC* (1981) 2 FLR 222 the House of Lords held that wardship is available to fill gaps or lacunae in the law. *A fortiori*, where no such gaps or lacunae exist it should not be available. However, in the light of the many recent commendations of wardship to local authorities by the High Court it seems most unlikely that it will be disallowed within the context of access appeals.

6.3.4 Supplementing local authority powers

It appears to be the case that whenever an authority are unhappy with their statutory powers or with the way in which a court has interpreted them it can invite the High Court to intervene via wardship. More specifically, the High Court's impressive array of powers may be attractive to the local authority, especially the flexible remedy of the injunction. For example, the court can grant an injunction against molestation of the child or a social worker by a parent, cf. *Re B (A Minor) (Wardship: Child in Care)* [1975] Fam. 36; or to prevent a child's removal from the jurisdiction, cf. *Re H(GJ) (An Infant)* [1966] 1 WLR 706; or to prevent a parent leaving the jurisdiction until the child's paternity has been established, *Re J (A Minor)* [1988] 1 FLR 65. It can entrust the ward to the care of X local authority notwithstanding the existence of a care order in favour of Y local authority, see *Re C (A Minor) (Wardship: Care Order)* (1983) 4 FLR 374. It can order that maintenance be paid for the ward, Family Law Reform Act 1969, s. 6 (as amended by the Family Law Reform Act 1987), and directly to the child where this is appropriate, Administration of Justice Act 1982, s. 50. The court's overriding concern for the welfare of the child enables it to grant injunctions designed to keep a child's circumstances confidential, for example by prohibiting the publication of a book, articles or reports about the child, *Re J (A Minor) (Wardship: Jurisdiction)* [1984] FLR 43; and see *Re X (A Minor) (Wardship: Jurisdiction* [1975] Fam. 47.

6.3.5 Cases of particular difficulty

Sometimes a case raises a difficult question of law or a matter of public importance, for example whether an operation to sterilize a child should be performed, *Re D (A Minor) (Wardship: Sterilization)* [1976] Fam. 185; *Re B* [1987] 2 FLR 314; or whether an abortion should be performed on a young girl in care against the wishes of her parents, *Re P (A Minor)* (1981) 80 LGR 301; or whether a life-saving operation should be performed on a handicapped baby against the wishes of her parents, *Re B (A Minor) (Wardship: Medical Treatment)* (1982) 3 FLR 117; or where a contract for surrogate parenthood is involved, *Re C (A Minor) (Wardship: Surrogacy)* [1985] FLR 846 *sub nom. Re A Baby*. The local authority may prefer to seek assistance in wardship rather than to rely on their statutory powers. Indeed these powers may be inappropriate to the circumstances; see, for example, the doubtful use of a place of safety order in *Re C (A Minor)* (above).

6.3.6 Sexual abuse

Controversy over the alleged incidence of sexual abuse of children and the diagnostic and evidential difficulties such cases raise warrant separate treatment, see §1.7. Indicative of these forensic difficulties is the fact that local authorities frequently prefer wardship to care proceedings in such cases, for signs of abuse may be ambiguous and fiercely disputed by expert witnesses.

6.3.7 The disadvantages of wardship to local authorities

Once the child is made a ward no important decision can be made about his upbringing without the matter first being referred back to a judge. For example, he cannot be placed for adoption without leave, *Re G (Wardship: Adoption)* (1981) 2 FLR 382, or be moved from short-term to long-term foster-parents without judicial approval, *Re CB (A Minor) (Wardship: Local Authority)* [1981] 1 WLR 379. The judge may decide that, in future, access will be controlled by the court rather than by the authority, *Re Y (A Minor)* [1985] FLR 294. On the other hand there are limits to this, and the court may be reluctant to constrain an authority too closely by instructing a specific course of action for a ward in their care, see *Surrey CC v W* (1982) 3 FLR 167.

Moreover, although wardship can be swiftly invoked, resolution of the case can be much delayed. The originating summons must be supported by affidavits, a preliminary hearing will take place before a registrar, further evidence such as reports from expert witnesses may be needed, and, if the Official Solicitor is asked to intervene, this will further delay the full hearing. Consequently wardship is not normally the quickest form of relief. Several months can easily pass. Indeed a place of safety order under s. 28 of the CYPA 1969 may well be needed in the interim to cope with urgent problems affecting the ward. In that case the High Court should be informed and directions sought, *Re B (A Minor)* (1980) 124 SJ 81. In the most extreme circumstances, where there is insufficient time to apply to the wardship court, the local authority may apply to the magistrates, without leave, for a place of safety order. In that case the local authority must inform the magistrates that the child is a ward and undertake to apply to the appropriate wardship court for further directions at the next sitting of the court and must so apply, *Practice Direction (Ward: Place of Safety)* [1988] 1 FLR 452. Furthermore, as every practitioner knows, action in the High Court is a costly business. For local authorities, in times of public expenditure stringency, the cost of two or three days in court, a possible appeal and all the preparatory work can be an important consideration.

6.4 When Wardship is Available to Parents or Third Parties

When it is recalled that a local authority possess most of the parental rights and duties in relation to a child in their care, the importance to the parent of obtaining a review of a local authority's decision can be appreciated. The local authority decide about access, placement with or removal from foster-parents, and the conditions in which a child is kept in institutional care. Decisions about access can be particularly significant. Where access is terminated, or substantially reduced, this often marks the first step in an authority's plan to sever the parental link and to provide the child with a permanent substitute home. During the 1960s and 1970s several attempts were made by parents and third parties to persuade judges to intervene in wardship to review the way in which local authorities had exercised their discretion. All such attempts failed on the ground that it is not the function of the High Court to control the exercise of a local authority's discretion (see particularly *Re M (An Infant)* [1961] Ch 328 and *Re W (Minors) (Wardship: Jurisdiction)* [1980] Fam. 60).

The question whether wardship is available to review a local authority's decision concerning a child in care first came before the House of Lords in 1981 in *A v Liverpool CC* (1981) 2 FLR 222.

There a mother sought to challenge the authority's decision to reduce her access from once a week to once a month. Their Lordships ruled that statute entrusts the care and control of children in care to local authorities, and that wardship must not be exercised so as to interfere with the day-to-day administration by authorities of that statutory control. In a second examination of the jurisdiction in *W* v *Hertfordshire CC* [1985] FLR 879 the House of Lords emphasized that the 'profoundly important' rule applies that:

'. . . where Parliament has by statute entrusted to a public authority an administrative power subject to safeguards which, however, contain no provision that the High Court is to be required to review the merits of decisions taken pursuant to the power, the High Court has no right to intervene.'

For a brief period after *A* v *Liverpool CC* (above) it appeared that wardship would still be available as an alternative to judicial review (see *D* v *X CC (No. 1)* [1985] FLR 275). But (in our view unfortunately) even this limited access to wardship has been denied to parents and others in the face of abuse of power, *Re DM* [1986] 2 FLR 122; *Re S (A Minor)* [1987] 1 FLR 479; *Re RM and LM* [1986] 2 FLR 205; *Re Y (Minors)* [1988] 1 FLR 299. Here it was firmly stated that any challenge to the way in which a local authority are exercising their child-care powers must be channelled through an application in judicial review (see §6.5).

6.4.1 Can wardship pre-empt the statutory code?

Is there any advantage to the parent or third party in instituting wardship proceedings where the local authority intend to act under the statutory code? The answer is 'no' because the High Court will decline jurisdiction, see *W* v *Shropshire CC* [1986] 1 FLR 359. Once preliminary steps have been taken, for example, a place of safety order has been obtained, or even when no proceedings have been commenced, but where an authority intend to take them, the statutory code prevails, *Re T (A Minor)* (1982) 12 Fam. Law 218; *Re E (Minors) (Wardship: Jurisdiction)* (1983) 4 FLR 668; *W* v *Nottinghamshire CC* [1986] 1 FLR 565.

6.4.2 Where a local authority waive their objection

The only case where wardship can be invoked by a parent or third party is where the local authority waive their objection. Thus if the authority agree with the wardship application and join in making it, the High Court will accept jurisdiction even though the authority have ample statutory powers to deal with the situation, see *A* v *B and Hereford and Worcester CC* [1986] 1 FLR 289. Conversely, if the local authority prefer to rely on those powers, the wardship application is doomed. Given the expense of wardship proceedings, the practitioner may find it difficult to persuade the authority to agree to an application. However, he may succeed in cases of complexity, or where there is evidence of equivocal and misleading social work practice which demands resolution by a High Court judge (for an example see *Re Y (A Minor)* [1985] FLR 294). Occasionally a judge will invite an authority to allow the wardship to continue by consent, see *Re S (A Minor)* (1981) 11 Fam. Law 175, or, when hearing an application for leave to apply for judicial review, he might add a recommendation that wardship proceedings be instituted, *R* v *Newham LBC* [1988] 1 FLR 416. It can be pointed out to the authority that their primary duty is to safeguard the welfare of the child and that sometimes this coincides with the use of wardship; also, that wardship is consistent with maintaining a policy of public accountability.

A local authority may be willing to allow parents to invoke wardship to secure the committal of their child to care where the child has reached the age of seventeen, see *Re SW (A Minor) (Wardship: Jurisdiction)* [1986] 1 FLR 24. Here the protective frameworks of the CYPA 1969 and the CCA 1980 no longer apply, whereas wardship is available until eighteen. Such cases will be rare and the remedy is of course only temporary.

6.4.3 When the child has been made a ward

It is most important that parents and others realize that once the child has been made a ward the High Court is in control. No important decision can be made in the child's life by the local authority or anyone else without the Court's consent. Occasionally a local authority will fail to observe this rule, see for example, *Re CB (A Minor)* [1981] 1 WLR 379; *Re El-G (Minors)* (1983) 4 FLR 421. Occasionally a local authority will deliberately not comply with the judge's ruling, see *Re D (A Minor)* [1987] 2 FLR 365. Sometimes this will be seriously prejudicial to parents and other interested persons. Lawyers representing such persons should be alert to this, should advise their clients to seek legal advice should such a situation arise, and should seek to get the wardship proceedings restored swiftly as time is often of the essence in cases of this type. The court may choose to mark its disapproval of what the local authority have done by awarding costs against them, *Havering LBC* v *S* [1986] 1 FLR 489.

6.5 Judicial Review

The demise of wardship as a remedy for anyone other than a local authority means that attention must be focused on judicial review as the primary method of challenging a local authority's actions. Anyone with sufficient interest in the matter can apply to the High Court for leave to seek judicial review of a decision made by an inferior court or a body charged with a public duty such as a local authority or an adoption agency, Supreme Court Act 1981, s. 31. The procedure and the scope of the remedy are set out in RSC Ord. 53. In a child-care case it would be normal for the court, on granting leave, to order that the case be entered on the expedited list.

Leave to apply for judicial review must be sought and it is at this first hurdle that many actions will founder. For, crucially, the judge will not grant leave on the basis that evidence of misconduct will come to light later during the process of discovery. Instead the applicant must produce sufficient cogent evidence at this preliminary stage so as to warrant pursuance of the remedy. It is thus essential to frame the terms of the application carefully.

6.5.1 Grounds for review

The grounds for judicial review were summarized by Lord Diplock in *Council of Civil Service Unions* v *Minister for the Civil Service* [1985] AC 374 under three heads, namely illegality, procedural impropriety and irrationality.

6.5.2 Illegality

Illegality consists of an error of law on the part of the decision-maker. It could arise, for example, where the local authority exercise a power which they do not have, such as keeping a child in care under s. 2 of the CCA 1980 against the parents' express wish to take charge of the child, or unilaterally changing a child's name or religion (powers which are specifically excluded from the parental rights which pass to an authority), or by keeping the child in secure accommodation when they have no power to do so. Illegality can arise where a court or an authority misconstrue their powers. Thus in *R* v *Bolton MBC ex parte B* [1985] FLR 343 an order of mandamus was granted where a local authority had misunderstood the meaning of s. 12B of the CCA 1980 (see §5.5.2).

Illegality can also occur where a local authority abuse their powers by using them for an improper purpose. For example, foster-parents who have looked after a child for three years can apply for a custodianship order and, whilst their application is pending, no one can remove the child from their care (Children Act 1975, s. 41; a similar provision exists after five years for an adoption application, Adoption Act 1976, s. 28). If a local authority learn of the foster-parents' intention to make an application and remove the child from their care solely so as to pre-empt the application, this could amount to an abuse of power such as to warrant judicial review, see the observations of Sheldon J in *Re RM and LM* [1986] 2 FLR 205. Similarly in *R* v *Bolton MBC ex parte B* [1985] FLR 343 mandamus was directed against a local authority which had wrongly delayed notifying the termination of parental access so that the access dispute could instead be dealt with in pending adoption proceedings. Another example of illegality is where a local authority fetter their discretion for handling individual cases by adopting a rigid policy; for example, by deciding never to take care proceedings for truancy against fourteen and fifteen-year-old children, or never to place coloured children with white foster-parents or vice versa, or never to use s. 1 of the CCA 1980 to help families found to be intentionally homeless under the Housing Act 1985 (see *Attorney-General ex rel Tilley* v *Wandsworth LBC* (1981) 2 FLR 377).

An authority can adopt a general policy on such matters but they must consider each case and be prepared to permit exceptions to the general policy. There are two particular difficulties in using judicial review here. First, it may be impossible or very difficult to obtain sufficient evidence of illegality. Secondly, if successful, the action in judicial review would require the authority to make a decision afresh. Provided they did so by properly considering each case, the result for the particular litigant might well be the same. However, the publicity which the action may generate may in turn bring helpful pressures on the authority; and the delay caused may help the merits of the applicant's case (for example, in the illustration above where white foster-parents have been allowed to keep the coloured child whilst the authority's policy is being challenged). Moreover, the judge hearing the judicial review application may be moved to suggest to the authority that they agree to submit to the wardship jurisdiction, cf *R* v *Newham LBC* [1988] 1 FLR 416.

6.5.3 Procedural impropriety

Procedural impropriety occurs where the local authority fail to observe either procedural rules set down by statute or the common-law requirements of natural justice and procedural fairness. The former is illustrated by the facts of *D* v *X CC (No. 1)* [1985] FLR

275 and *Re S* [1987] 1 FLR 479, which concerned the failure of a local authority to notify interested persons of pending care proceedings, contrary to the notice requirements of the CYP Rules 1988. The limitation of judicial review in this context is that a rehearing of the care proceedings, after proper notice has been given, is unlikely to help the aggrieved third party for a juvenile court can make a limited range of orders and cannot, for example, give care and control of the child to a third party. The advantages of wardship for a third party are self-evident but *Re S* (above) has clearly stated that it is unavailable in these circumstances.

Another example of procedural impropriety was offered by *Re L (AC)* [1971] 3 All ER 743 where a local authority misled a parent about her right to object to a resolution passed under s. 3 of the CCA 1980 and failed to observe the proper procedures for the assumption of parental rights; see also *Re S (A Minor)* (1981) 11 Fam. Law 175. In this type of case judicial review might not be so fruitless, for at a rehearing on the parental rights resolution the burden of proof would lie on the local authority to justify the resolution (see §2.5.1) and the parent might thus succeed on the merits in defeating the resolution.

Procedural impropriety also includes the failure to observe the common-law requirements of natural justice. This can arise both outside and inside the courtroom. As to the former, natural justice requires a local authority to reach decisions about a child without personal bias against a parent. Hence the importance of involving other professionals and a more senior social workers than the case worker in the decision-making process is self-evident. Natural justice also requires an authority to give the parent an opportunity of hearing and dealing with serious allegations made against him. For example, in *R v Bedfordshire CC ex parte C* [1987] 1 FLR 239, as a result of the mother making unsubstantiated allegations of sexual misconduct against the father, the local authority reversed their earlier decision to return the child home to the father on a trial basis. Certiorari was granted and the authority were ordered to allow the father to make appropriate representations before a fresh decision on the child's future was taken. The scope of this decision is quite narrow when the facts of *R v Hertfordshire CC ex parte B* [1987] 1 FLR 239 are considered. There the local authority's decision not to return a child to the mother for a trial period was based on several factors, only one of which was an allegation of drunkenness made by a neighbour against the mother. It was held that natural justice did not require that the mother be given an opportunity to meet the allegation. The result of these two cases would appear to be that the opportunity to rebut an allegation of misconduct will only be necessary if that allegation is the sole evidence against the person. This distinction is harsh. Moreover, since parents are not usually allowed to attend case conferences (indeed the 1986 DHSS guide, para. 2.25, states that 'it is not appropriate for parents to attend inter-agency case conferences'), it may be quite fortuitous that the allegation comes to the parents' notice. It thus behoves the participants at case conferences and other meetings to adhere to the requirements of natural justice and to ensure that evidence against parents and others is rigorously tested.

As for natural justice within the courtroom, the CYP Rules 1988 spell out the minimal requirements (such as the right of parties to meet allegations made against them or to hear a summary of the evidence given in their absence from the courtroom) and have also come to recognize the role which grandparents and others can and ought to play in the proceedings. Consequently the common law has a limited role to play. But, as *R* v *West Malling Juvenile Court ex parte K* [1986] 2 FLR 405 indicates, the duty to act fairly means that serious evidence against a party should not be delivered 'at the door of the court' but should be disclosed sufficiently in advance for a proper response to be formulated.

6.5.4 Irrationality or unreasonableness

Irrationality or unreasonableness encompasses what have become known as the 'Wednesbury principles' after *Associated Provincial Picture Houses Ltd* v *Wednesbury Corporation* [1948] 1 KB 223. They allow a decision to be attacked in judicial review in the following circumstances. First, where a decision has been reached on irrelevant considerations, for example, where a social worker is shown to have been motivated by personal spite against a parent, or an authority has mistreated foster-parents for political, racial, or other reasons which are irrelevant to the child's welfare. Secondly, where a decision-maker has ignored relevant considerations; for example, *Re B (Child in Care: Wardship)* (1981) 2 FLR 412 where a child was placed for adoption without considering the views of a psychiatrist who favoured the natural mother; and *Re D (A Minor)* (1979) JSWL 107 where a parental rights resolution had been based on an inadequate agenda note.

The difficulty in establishing either of these grounds lies, of course, in discovering the factors which influenced the authority. Some assistance in this regard can be found in the observations of the Court of Appeal in the context of education where it was stated by the Master of the Rolls that:

'if the allegation is that a decision is prima facie irrational and that there are grounds for inquiring whether something immaterial may have been considered or something material omitted from consideration, it really does not help to assert boldly that all relevant matters and no irrelevant matters were taken into consideration without condescending to mention some at least of the principal factors on which the decision was based.' *R v Lancashire CC ex parte Huddleston* [1986] 2 All ER 941.

Thirdly, a decision may be attacked where it is so irrational or unreasonable that no reasonable person could have arrived at it. This is a most difficult ground to establish, for the local authority are being challenged, not for a specific incident of wrongdoing, but for the overall impression of wrongness. Allied to this is the general unwillingness (illustrated by the cases on wardship, see §6.4) of courts to intervene in the daily actions of local authorities. An example of the hurdles facing judicial review in this category is *Re DM* [1986] 2 FLR 122 where foster-parents had cared for a very young child for eight months, had become deeply attached to him, and had asked to be considered as adoptive parents. The natural mother objected on the ground that she did not wish to know the identity of her child's adoptive parents. The adoption panel rejected the foster-parents, though the mother's views were *not* taken into account in reaching that decision. The foster-parents could see no good reason for their rejection but, because they failed to establish 'any impropriety or fundamental error in principle', relief in judicial review would have been denied (see p. 131, per Purches LJ). If this uncompromising stance is maintained by the Court of Appeal, a challenge under this head of judicial review will prove extremely difficult. The lawyer representing disgruntled parents will be forced either to search for a specific tangible sign of error on the authority's part or to amass such overwhelming evidence (preferably from expert witnesses) as to prove that the authority have acted unreasonably; cf. *Re H* [1985] FLR 519 where it was stated, *obiter*, that if a social worker were to remove a child from foster-parents, with whom he had lived for seven years, against the near unanimous opposition of those with direct knowledge of the child, the decision might be challengeable. Similarly, if a local authority remove a child from foster-parents in order solely to pre-empt the latter's application for custodianship (after three years) or adoption (after five years), the authority's decision could be challenged as being so unreasonable that no reasonable authority would act in similar fashion, see *Re RM and LM* [1986] 2 FLR 205. If, on the other hand, the authority intervened after two years and eleven months, *Re DM* (above) indicates that considerable evidence of harm to the child's welfare would have to be amassed before the apparent lawfulness of the decision could be successfully challenged. It is suggested that, in such a case where there appears to be no good reason for a decision, the local authority should be more forthcoming in disclosing their reasons for a decision (see the observations in *R v Lancashire CC ex parte Huddleston* (above)). The DHSS Circular on Personal Social Services Records, LAC (83) 14, encouraging more openness from local authorities in respect of case records and the observations of the European Court of Human Rights (below, §6.8) stressing respect for family life and procedural fairness, are factors which may assist this suggestion.

6.5.5 Remedies in judicial review

The foregoing grounds for judicial review can overlap and in some cases more than one ground can be invoked, cf. *Re L (AC) (An Infant)* [1971] 3 All ER 743. It should be noted that the potential scope for judicial review is tempered by the judiciary's reluctance to interfere with those daily, frequently difficult, and in some respects impressionistic, decisions which Parliament has entrusted to public bodies; see the attitude adopted in the wardship context in *A v Liverpool CC* (1981) 2 FLR 222 and *W v Hertfordshire CC* [1985] FLR 879 and compare *R v Hillingdon LBC ex parte Puhlhofer* [1986] 2 WLR 259 (in relation to housing) and *R v Secretary of State for the Home Department ex parte Swati* [1986] 1 WLR 477 (in relation to immigration).

If an application for judicial review succeeds, the court can grant the remedies of certiorari, mandamus, prohibition, declaration, injunction and damages. However, it must be stressed that the award of a remedy is a matter for the discretion of the court (see, for example, *R v Chertsey Justices ex parte E* [1987] 2 FLR 415) and the court may well take the view that a remedy is inappropriate, for example, because of the passage of time since the proven unlawfulness, or because, even if the local authority had behaved correctly, the result for the particular child would have been the same, or because the authority's error was a technicality compared with the child's future welfare. The most serious drawback to the remedies available in judicial review is that the merits of a decision cannot be challenged. Judicial review cannot afford the complainant the remedy he really seeks, namely a fresh and independent review of the decision. The most that the court can do is to quash the decision and to remit the matter to the decision-maker. It is then relatively easy for the local authority to reconsider properly but still reach the same decision on the merits, whilst it may be very difficult for the

complainant to accept that the fresh decision has been made imparti-
ally. The advantages of wardship in this context are self-evident but,
as has been seen, that avenue of relief has been firmly closed.

6.6 Habeas Corpus

An application for a writ of habeas corpus is made by a child's parent
or guardian to a judge of the Family Division (Administration of
Justice Act 1970, s. 1 (2) and Sch. 1) and by any other person to any
High Court judge. The use of habeas corpus in child-custody cases
has been regarded as unsuitable, see *Re K (A Minor)* (1978) LSG
711, for the lawfulness of the detention is the question before the
court rather than the welfare of the child, and clearly release of the
child may not serve his best interests. Thus judicial review must
normally be the more appropriate remedy. However, habeas corpus
proceedings will be heard very quickly, and it is suggested that with
the unavailability of wardship as a remedy (see §6.5) and in the face
of a blatantly unlawful detention, for example, where foster-parents
refuse to deliver up a child or to tell a local authority where the child
is, or where an authority refuse to return a child from voluntary care
in the face of a parent's repeated demands, such proceedings are the
appropriately swift remedy, for even on habeas corpus the welfare
of the child must be considered, cf. *Re AB (An Infant)* [1954] 2 QB
385. At the very least, a writ of habeas corpus can be threatened
against the detainer.

6.7 The Local Ombudsman

An individual can complain to the local ombudsman, the Commissioner for Local Administration, about injustice sustained in consequence of maladministration by a local authority. The complaint must
be made via a member of the authority or, if he refuses to forward
it, directly to the Commissioner. For the scope of the jurisdiction see
Part III of the Local Government Act 1973. The remedy can be a
useful outlet for a parent who is disgruntled at the way in which a
local authority have treated him, but whose complaints do not warrant
judicial remedies. Moreover, whether or not a complaint is upheld,
the observations of the Commissioner can prompt reform of a local
authority's practices. Thus, resort to the Commissioner can be useful
if the local authority act with undue haste in passing a s. 3 resolution
under the CCA 1980 and without proper internal consultation (for
example, between the Director of the Social Services Department

and the chairman of the local authority's Social Services Committee), or without external consultation between the authority and the parent, especially if the latter has been led to believe that a local authority will not seek to gain permanent care of the child, see complaint number *221/YU/83* against Ealing LBC (9 May 1984).

In some cases urgent action by the local authority is not required to protect the child, and the authority will enter into discussions with a parent. If the authority then fail to keep the parent informed of their thinking and suddenly announce plans for the adoption of the child, the manner of their decision-making can be investigated by the local ombudsman, even though the merits of the decision cannot be, see complaint number *547/J/81* against Hereford and Worcester CC (28 February 1983). Complaints to the local ombudsman can also assist third parties such as grandparents or foster-parents. For example, foster-parents can allege that they have been improperly withdrawn from the list of approved foster-parents. Again, if a care order is discharged and the child is removed from the possession of the foster-parents, the foster-parents may naturally be disturbed. If the child is subsequently readmitted to the local authority's care, but the original foster-parents are denied care of, or access to, the child, their grievance is even more understandable. It may then be possible to criticize the local authority's conduct, for example, for failure to consider the interests of the foster-parents, or failure to monitor the child's development properly during his stay with the natural parents, compare the facts of complaint number *857/C/81* against Rochdale MBC (23 August 1983).

All the examples illustrate that the practitioner must acquire a working knowledge of any local codes of practice or guidelines governing social work practice. If he does, he is much more able to gauge the propriety of the conduct. There are, however, three severe limitations to the ombudsman's usefulness. First, his investigation tends to be lengthy and thus quite unsuited to the immediacy of most individual child-care problems. Secondly, he is confined to investigating maladministration: for example, neglect, unreasonable delay in dealing with matters, misleading statements or incorrect advice to members of the public, or arbitrary or perverse action. This means that the ombudsman cannot deal with the merits of a particular decision. Thirdly, his findings cannot at the end of the day be enforced. He can merely issue a second adverse report against the recalcitrant local authority.

6.8 European Convention for the Protection of Human Rights and Fundamental Freedoms

Resort to the European Commission, and thereafter the European Court of Human Rights, is increasingly common today in cases where the laws of the United Kingdom are believed to fall short of the basic requirements set out in the Convention. Thus in *O, W, B, H* and *R* v *UK* 1987, Judgments vols. 120–1, parents objected to the behaviour of local authorities, in particular to the denial of access to their children whilst they were in local authority care. The European Court found in their favour, ruling that the right to a family life (article 8) had been unjustifiably infringed, and ultimately awarded damages of between £5,000 and £12,000. In the meantime one gap in UK law revealed by the judgments (access to children in care) was remedied by the Health and Social Security and Social Services Adjudications Act 1983 (now Part 1A of the CCA 1980, see chapter 5). The European Court has also responded to the Convention on the Legal Status of Children born out of Wedlock (1975), by denouncing the legal disabilities facing illegitimate children (*Johnston* v *Ireland* 1986, Judgment vol. 112; *Inze* v *Austria* 1987, Judgment vol. 126) and, as will be seen in chapter 7, the Family Law Reform Act 1987 has been the United Kingdom's response. Indeed the European Commission and Court have shown a growing interest in family law in recent years; for example, in the immigration context by stressing the need to maintain family life (see *Abdulaziz, Cabales and Balkandali* v *UK* 1985, Judgment vol. 94, *Berrehab* v *Netherlands* 1988, Judgment vol. 138), in the way in which troublesome juveniles are placed in remand prisons (*Bouamar* v *Belgium* 1988, Judgment vol. 129) and in the availability of decrees of divorce and judicial separation (*Airey* v *Ireland* 1979, Judgment vol. 32; *F* v *Switzerland* 1987, Judgment vol. 128). In the child-care context, the European Court has ruled that the splitting up of siblings and the placing of them at unduly far distances from their parents, thus making access difficult, may contradict the ultimate aim of reunification of the family and may therefore be an unjustifiable intrusion into family life (*Olsson* v *Sweden* 1988, Judgment vol. 130). In *H* v *UK* (above) the Court has stressed the need for urgency in wardship proceedings and that excessive delay in deciding a child's future could contribute to a breach of article 8 (right to private and family life). In similar vein in *B* v *UK* (above) the Court has urged the need for local authorities to involve parents in the decision-making process. Whilst in 1988 in *Gaskin* v *UK* Application No. 10454/83 (European Commission) the Court has been asked to decide upon the extent to which an individual is entitled to see his social services case-file (the applicant having failed to secure discovery in English law) and the judgment is awaited. Further development in the procedural field could lie in the protection of relatives such as uncles, aunts, brothers or sisters who are very close to the child but who are not sufficiently catered for in the CYP Rules 1988, or of persons such as grandparents or foster-parents who are mentioned in the Rules but whose involvement in the proceedings is narrowly confined by the particular juvenile court. As for the substantive law, it must be questioned whether a ground for care proceedings in the CYPA 1969 such as 'moral danger' is sufficiently precise so as to warrant an interference with 'family life' in accordance with article 8(2) of the European Convention. The most relevant articles of the Convention by which current and future laws can be judged are articles 6 (the right to a fair hearing in the determination of a person's civil rights and obligations), 8 (right to private and family life) and 13 (right to an effective remedy for violation of one's rights).

At the national level the Convention may have a useful supporting role to play in the future. In a legal context where concern for children's welfare predominates, courts may be more willing to hear argument on the Convention's substance and more reluctant to hear technical points about the constitutional status of the Convention, compare the approach of the House of Lords in *Re KD (A Minor)* [1988] 2 FLR 139 with the more negative attitude displayed by the House in *Re M and H (Minors)* [1988] 3 WLR 485.

7 THIRD PARTIES

7.1 Introduction

In addition to parents and guardians, many other people can have an interest in the welfare of a child and may wish to have this interest considered by a local authority and ultimately a court. Such people can be described as third parties and they have appeared in passing throughout this book. In this chapter their legal position is considered separately, and across the spectrum of child-care law. They include grandparents, siblings, other more remote relatives, step-parents, foster-parents and even concerned strangers. Moreover, since the law narrowly prescribes who are to be parties to proceedings in child care, the phrase 'third parties' is wide enough to include a biological parent such as a non-custodial parent or the father of an illegitimate child. It is this broader definition which is employed in this chapter. As will be seen the law gives slightly more legal redress to the parent third party than to the non-parent third party and grandparents are afforded special consideration.

At the outset it should be noted that there is often a difference between the provisions of the law and good social work practice. The law has conceded only a limited status to third parties in judicial proceedings, whilst social workers have the power to consult with anyone who has a genuine interest in the welfare of a child, and to take his or her views into account. This means that third parties will wish to resolve a dispute over the future of a child within a legal framework only when relationships within the social work framework have broken down and a conflict cannot be resolved by discussion and compromise. Indeed, it should always be borne in mind that a local authority have very considerable powers with respect to children in care, that a court will normally be loath to intervene in the way in which those powers are exercised, and that conciliation and nego-tiation are likely to achieve better results than litigation for third parties.

7.1.1 Social work practice and the wider family

Enshrined in statute and central to good social work practice is the principle that in reaching any decision relating to a child in their care, a local authority shall give first consideration to the need to safeguard and promote the welfare of the child throughout his childhood, CCA 1980, s. 18. Interpretation of this principle can lead local authorities to give varying weight to the value of the child maintaining his links with his wider family and friends. Some authorities make strenuous efforts to preserve relationships, however tenuous; others operate no particular policy about the wider family; others take the view that a child's need for protection and security often requires him to be placed with a permanent substitute family, and all his links with his natural family to be severed. Whatever their preferred approach it is not only inappropriate but also an unlawful fettering of their discretion for an authority to adopt a single policy in relation to all the children in their care. Their ages, circumstances and experience range from newborn infants to teenagers on the threshold of adulthood. The importance to be attached to a child maintaining his family links will consequently vary considerably.

7.2 Voluntary Care

When a child is in voluntary care under s. 2 of the CCA 1980, legislative policy directs the local authority to endeavour to secure that the care of the child is taken over either by a parent or guardian of his, or by a relative or friend of his, where this is consistent with the welfare of the child, s. 2 (3). Where a relative or other interested person is willing to offer a home to a child who is presently in voluntary care, and where this offer has been ignored or rejected by the local authority, it may prove helpful to ask the authority to explain why they have chosen to depart from general legislative policy. A letter to the Director of Social Services, or to the chairman of the Social Services Committee, along these lines may promote reconsideration of the matter. However, it should be remembered that the decision whether to place a child with a relative or friend rests entirely with the local authority, and that the duty to do so arises only where the authority are satisfied that this would be consistent with the child's welfare. The statute provides no mechanism for a review of the decision by the courts; and the High Court will not intervene in wardship to override a discretion conferred by statute on a local authority and properly exercised, *W v Hertfordshire CC* [1985] FLR 879; *Re C(A) (An Infant)* [1966] 1 WLR 415. If the discretion is unlawfully exercised (for example, a social worker rejects a relative out of spite) judicial review may be available (see §6.5).

Access to a child in voluntary care is also controlled by the local authority, and there are no formal proceedings in which a non-parent can challenge a denial of access. However, a solicitor's letter, to the effect that it is generally accepted to be good social work practice to involve the child's wider family in his care and upbringing, might assist the person aggrieved in his negotiations with the authority. Reference to para. 8 of the *Code of Practice on Access to Children in Care* (see chapter 5), issued by the DHSS, might be made. This states:

'Considerations of access should take into account the child's wider family. The access arrangements should include relatives – siblings, grandparents, putative fathers for example – with whom contact should be preserved. In some cases it may be helpful to identify relatives, who may include a non-custodial parent, with whom contact has lapsed and to follow up the prospects of re-establishing contact. Care will clearly be needed where there is family or marital conflict, but authorities should be ready to explore possibilities of preserving and establishing contacts and of promoting access which will be beneficial to the child.'

7.2.1 Voluntary care and 'third-party parents'

A parent or guardian has the right to remove a child from voluntary care without notice when the child has been in care for less than six months; after six months have elapsed 28 days' notice in writing must be given (see §§2.1–2.2). It is thus important to know whether the third party qualifies in law as a 'parent' or 'guardian'. If he does not, he must take other steps to acquire that legal status before he can exercise statutory rights in respect of a child in voluntary care.

7.2.2 Definition of a 'parent' or 'guardian'

'Parent' is defined by s. 87 (1) of the CCA 1980 as the mother and father of a legitimate child, but the mother only of an illegitimate child. The status of the putative father is complex. Under the Family Law Reform Act 1987 (FLRA) he is recognized as a parent for certain purposes under the Child Care Act 1980, but not for those significant provisions under Part I and ss. 13, 24, 64 and 65 which concern reception into care, assumption of parental rights and duties by local authorities and voluntary organisations, and the power to arrange for a child's emigration. It is only when an order is in force under s. 4 of the FLRA 1987, by virtue of which actual custody is shared between the mother and father, that the putative father will be treated as a parent under the above provisions, CCA 1980, s. 8 (3). It is suggested that it is unlikely that many fathers will have the foresight to apply for such orders.

'Guardian' is defined as a person appointed by deed or will or by an order of a court of competent jurisdiction to be the guardian of a child. Both definitions are qualified by s. 8 (2) which provides that, where an order of any court is in force giving the right to the actual custody of a child to any person, that person only is the child's 'parent' or 'guardian' for the purposes of ss. 1–7 of the CCA 1980.

These narrow definitions can exclude a child's biological mother or father from their scope. In particular, where a custody order has been made, a non-custodial parent has no status under significant provisions of the CCA 1980; importantly, he has no right to remove his child from care under s. 2 (3). In the following paragraph it is assumed that the non-custodial parent is the husband.

7.2.3 The non-custodial spouse

If a non-custodial husband wishes to remove his child from s. 2 care, but the local authority refuse to permit this, what can he do? The first and most obvious step is to persuade the mother to exercise her right under s. 2 (3) to take the child from care (after giving 28 days' notice where this is required, see §2.1.4) and to place the child with him. Where the local authority, out of concern for the welfare of the child, object to this course of action, they should immediately take steps to prevent removal, either by assuming the mother's parental rights under s. 3, or by instituting wardship proceedings (see §§2.3.1 and 6.4.2).

If the mother will not agree to this proposal, the next logical step open to the husband is to apply for a variation of the existing custody order as against the mother (and see *R* v *Oxford City Justices ex parte H* [1975] QB 1). However, as soon as it emerges that the child is in local authority care the court is almost certain to decline to hear the case in the light of the House of Lords' ruling in *Re M and H (Minors)* [1988] 3 WLR 485. Here it was stated that a court should refuse to adjudicate on the merits of a custody application when a child is in care, despite having jurisdiction to do so. Arguably, voluntary care is distinguishable from a case where the local authority have parental rights (the position in *Re M and H (Minors)*) because the mother has retained all parental rights so that, logically, she, not the authority, is respondent to the action. In the unlikely event that a court is persuaded by this argument and agrees to adjudicate on the merits, it is bound to ask for a welfare report. In the light of that report the court may well consider it is in the child's best interests to remain in care, in which case it can either refuse to give custody to the father, or rule that there are exceptional circumstances making it impracticable or undesirable for the child to be entrusted to either of the parents or to any other individual, so that it can exercise its power to commit the child to the care of the local authority, Guardianship Act 1973, s. 2 (2) (*b*); Domestic Proceedings and Magistrates' Courts Act 1978, s. 10 (1); Matrimonial Causes Act 1973, s. 43 (1). Where the court is persuaded that the child's best interests are better served if he goes to live with his father, it can give custody to the father. He will then be in the position to assert his right to remove his child from care under s. 2 (3) of the CCA 1980.

It will be regrettable if in the light of *Re M and H (Minors)*, courts automatically decline jurisdiction in cases of this kind, for in some situations the authority may have formed the opinion that the child should live with the father, but have been dissuaded from placing the child with him because of hostility to this proposal from the custodial wife. Suggesting to the father that he consider applying for custody is one way in which the authority can resolve their dilemma; the responsibility for any decision to place the child with the father will then be for the court, and existing good social work relationships with the mother will not necessarily be jeopardized.

7.2.4 The putative father

The putative father's position appears to be similar. It has been seen that normally he has no parental rights under Part I of the CCA 1980 (unless he has obtained a parental rights order under FLR 1987, see §7.2.2). However, he has the right to apply for legal custody of his child under the Guardianship of Minors Act 1971 (GMA), ss. 9 and 14, *R v Oxford City Justices ex parte H* [1975] QB 1; *Re M and H (Minors)* [1988] 3 WLR 485. But he too must circumvent the ruling in *Re M and H (Minors)*. If the mother can be persuaded to support an agreed custody order, it may never emerge that the child is in voluntary care, for it is suggested that the respondent to any such application must be the mother, not the local authority. For, despite the fact that the child is in care, the parental rights remain vested in the mother and they must therefore be transferred from her. Armed with a custody order, the father is now in the position to request to take over the care of his child under s. 2 (3) of the CCA 1980. The local authority can, of course, resist this manoeuvre, either by warding the child or, where there are grounds, by assuming the father's parental rights under s. 3 of the CCA 1980. In the more probable event that the adjudicating court is informed that the child is in care, it is likely to decline to exercise its custody jurisdiction (see §7.2.3).

7.3 Where the Local Authority have Assumed Parental Rights

When a child is in care under s. 2 of the CCA 1980, the local authority can assume the parental rights of each parent by a resolution made under s. 3, provided that there are grounds for doing so (see §2.3). When the parental rights of only one parent have been assumed, s. 3 (1) provides that the parental rights shall be vested in the authority jointly with the other parent. It is suggested that this other parent retains all the rights of a parent of a child in s. 2 care only, in particular, the right to remove his child from care under s. 2 (3). If it transpires that his intention is to place the child in the same household as the parent whose rights have been assumed, that in itself gives the local authority the power to assume his parental rights, s. 3 (1) (c). Otherwise, where the authority wish to keep the child in care, they must either assume his parental rights on one of the other grounds, or have recourse to wardship.

7.3.1 The non-custodial spouse

The matter is complicated when there is a court order in force giving the custody of a child to a person. Only that person is recognized as the child's 'parent' for the purpose of the CCA 1980, ss. 1–7, and the natural parent loses his parental status, s. 8 (2). Consequently, the local authority need only assume the parental rights of the person with custody, and should not concern themselves with any non-custodial parent. This means that the non-custodial parent (the father, for the purposes of the following discussion) cannot object to the assumption of parental rights by the authority and force the authority to take proceedings in the juvenile court under s. 3 (5); he cannot apply to have the resolution determined under s. 5 (4); and he has no right to remove the child from care under s. 2 (3). The only step the father can take is to apply for a variation of the custody order in custody proceedings but this will not assist him because the court may not review the manner in which an authority are exercising their powers and duties in respect of a child in care over whom they have parental rights. The court must therefore decline to exercise its custody jurisdiction (*Re M and H (Minors)* [1988] 3 WLR 485).

Accordingly, the non-custodial parent appears to have no remedy despite such an approach probably being in breach of the European Convention for the Protection of Human Rights and Fundamental Freedoms (see *Re M and H (Minors)* and §6.8).

7.3.2 The putative father

As to the natural father of an illegitimate child, he is in an identical position to a non-custodial parent. It was held in *R v Oxford City Justices ex parte H* [1975] QB 1; *Re M and H (Minors)* [1988] 3 WLR 485; *Re D (A Minor)* [1988] 2 FLR 106, that the assumption of the parental rights of the natural mother leaves untouched the father's right to apply for custody under ss. 9 and 14 of the GMA 1971. But the courts will nevertheless decline to hear a case on the merits.

7.3.3 Other third parties

When proceedings are brought under ss. 3 (6) or 5 (4) of the CCA 1980, a third party has a right to be notified of the proceedings when the child has had his home with him for a period of, or periods amounting in total to, not less than 42 days ending not more than six months before the date of the complaint, if the whereabouts of such a person are known to the local authority or voluntary organisation, CYP Rules 1988, r. 30. Such a person is entitled to make representations to the court at the conclusion of the evidence, r. 30 (3). Foster-parents in particular will benefit from this opportunity. However, it should be noted that this safeguard will normally be lost where termination of a parental rights resolution is unopposed by the local authority, for a parental rights resolution can be rescinded at any time by the authority, and it is unlikely that an unopposed application will come before the court.

7.4 Guardianship

In some situations the GMA 1971 offers relief for third parties. Section 5 (1) provides that where a child has no parent, no guardian and no other person having parental rights with respect to him, any person may apply to be appointed as the child's guardian. The scope of the provision is narrow, and the precise meaning of 'no other person having parental rights' obscure. Whether a natural father is classified as a parent turns on whether either an order is in force under the FLRA 1987, s. 4, giving him all the parental rights and duties with respect to the child (this provision is not yet in force), or whether he has a right to custody, legal or actual custody, or care and control of the child by virtue of an order made under any other enactment, GMA 1971, s. 5 (3). It should be noted that s. 5 (2) of the GMA 1971 specifically provides that the court may entertain an application for guardianship notwithstanding that a local authority have assumed parental rights by resolution under s. 3 of the CCA 1980; and s. 5 (2) (c) of the CCA 1980 states that if the court appoints a guardian the resolution ceases to have effect. Any attempt by the court to treat its jurisdiction as one limited by the non-intervention principles established in *A* v *Liverpool CC* (1981) 2 FLR 222; *W* v *Hertfordshire CC* [1985] FLR 879 (see §6.4); *Re M and H (Minors)* [1988] 3 WLR 485 (see §7.3.1) would therefore be misconceived and should be resisted strongly by the lawyer acting for the applicant. However, it is not clear whether an application for guardianship can be made in respect of an orphaned child committed to care by court order in matrimonial, guardianship or care proceedings. It is suggested that because a local authority do not obtain the entire bundle of parental rights vested in a parent or guardian when the court order is made (for example, the right to agree to the child's adoption and the right to alter his religion are both left untouched) a guardianship application may be permissible, as this enables the court to vest the full rights of guardianship in the applicant.

Section 5 (1) of the GMA 1971 can therefore prove invaluable to any third party who wishes to acquire parental rights over an orphaned child in care. It is particularly useful to a step-parent or relative because the court must examine the merits of the applicant's proposal, and its decision is dictated by the paramountcy of the child's welfare. It is suggested that a court might often decide that a member of an orphaned child's wider family should be given the status of guardian, so that he, rather than the local authority, can take over the powers and duties of the parent.

7.5 Rights of Audience in Care Proceedings

The CYP Rules 1988 accord various rights to parents, guardians, grandparents, foster-parents and other persons who have an interest in the outcome of care proceedings. The situation can vary between one where a parent, guardian or grandparent enjoys party status and one where the interested person has no rights in the proceedings. Sometimes the court must decide who should be accorded rights. It may also be necessary for the applicant to decide whether a person falls within the scope of the rules at the outset, for such a person may be entitled to notification of the proceedings under r. 14.

7.5.1 Definition of a 'parent'

As with the CCA 1980, the CYPA 1969 draws a distinction between parents who are married and those who are not. While, generally speaking, the FLRA 1987, s. 1 (1) requires relationships to be construed without regard to whether a child's parents are married, where a contrary intention appears this provision does not apply. Practitioners should note that s. 8 of the FLRA 1987 inserts such a contrary intention into the interpretation of s. 70 of the CYPA 1969. Section 70 (1A) states that any reference in the 1969 Act to the parent of a child includes, in the case of unmarried parents, the father where an order of any court is in force giving him the right to the actual custody of the child. In the absence of such an order, the mother is the sole parent. (Of course, s. 70 (1A) does not apply to fathers of legitimated or adopted children, s. 70 (1B).) However, where the putative father is living in a stable relationship with the child's mother, niceties of status which turn on the child's legitimacy or illegitimacy are out of place, and in practice the natural father is sometimes treated as the child's 'parent'. A step-parent is not a 'parent', but where he has acquired parental rights by order of a court, for example, in custody proceedings, it is suggested that he will fall within the definition of a 'guardian' (below). It is clear that a non-custodial parent retains his status for the purpose of proceedings brought under the CYPA 1969 even where custody has been given to the other parent, or to a third party, by a court order.

7.5.2 Definition of a 'guardian'

'Guardian' is generously defined. It includes any person who 'has for the time being charge or control over the child or young person', CYPA 1969, s. 70 (2); and CYPA 1933, s. 107 (1). There is no authority on the proper interpretation of this phrase. It is suggested that a court will normally only recognize a third party as the child's guardian either in a case where the parent is not exercising parental rights over the child or in a case where the parent and third party are exercising parental rights jointly. An obvious example is where the child's parents are unmarried but living together; here the father will fall within the definition of a guardian. In *Humberside CC v DPR* [1977] 1 WLR 1251 it was accepted that the mother's cohabitee (but not the child's father) was the child's guardian. Rule 14 (3) (*b*) of the CYP Rules 1988 requires that the parent *or* guardian of the child must be notified of an application in care proceedings; the use of 'or' may mean that, provided the child's parent has been notified of the proceedings and attends the hearing, there is no duty on the court to accord guardian status to a third party who is looking after the child. However, justice and the spirit of the rules demand that both be informed and asked to attend. In addition to having the right to be notified of the application and to attend the hearing, a guardian is given the same rights of participation in the hearing as those accorded to a parent. These include the rights to represent the child, to separate legal representation, to legal aid, to cross-examine witnesses, to call evidence and to make representations to the court (see chapter 4). Whether a guardian is entitled to be accorded these rights when a parent is already exercising the same rights is unclear. Where their interests conflict this can be a very real issue, and one which the court may choose to resolve under its inherent jurisdiction to conduct its proceedings flexibly and in the interests of justice, see §1.2.

7.5.3 Persons with whom the child has had his home

A more limited right to participate in care proceedings is given to:

> 'any foster-parent or other person with whom the relevant infant has had his home for a period of, or periods amounting in total to, not less than 42 days, ending not more than six months before the date of the application, if the whereabouts of such a person is known to the applicant or can readily be, ascertained by him.'
> r. 14 (3) (*d*).

Such a person must be notified of the proceedings, and is entitled to attend the hearing and to make representations to the court at any stage after the conclusion of the evidence, r. 19 (1). The court may also allow copies of any report to be shown to him, r. 25 (2). Rule 14 (3) (*d*) was introduced as a result of the Maria Colwell tragedy and it applies whether the application is to make, or to discharge, an order. It is of special value to foster-parents who may wish to oppose an application to discharge a child from care. Not only can the foster-parents (or any other persons falling within the rule) be called as witnesses, they are also entitled to make their own independent representations to the court and put forward their own assessment of the child's long-term interests based on their special knowledge of the child's personality (for the procedural rules, see §4.5.1).

However, where the discharge of a care order is *not opposed* by the local authority, this safeguard for the child is usually lost. An increase in access visits followed by the placement of a child at home nearly always precedes any formal steps to discharge a child from care and the child will normally have been living at home for several months or even years before an application is made to the juvenile court. By the time any unopposed application is brought before the court, the foster-parents have usually stopped looking after the child long ago, and so fall outside r. 14 (3) (*d*). They may, however, have rights under r. 19 (3) (see §7.5.5).

On those few occasions when an unopposed application to discharge a care order is brought before magistrates while the child is still physically with foster-parents, or has only recently left their home, rr. 14 (3) (*d*) and 19 (1) have particular value to the foster-parents. On being notified of the application, foster-parents who wish to oppose it should immediately inform the court. The court must then order that no parent shall be treated as representing the child or as otherwise authorized to act on his behalf, unless satisfied that to do so is not necessary for safeguarding the interests of the child, CYPA 1969, s. 32A (2). Furthermore, the court must appoint a guardian ad litem of the child, unless satisfied that to do so is not necessary for safeguarding the child's interests, s. 32B (1). When, therefore, the court learns that there is opposition to the application from quarters other than the local authority, a separate representation order should be made and a guardian ad litem appointed. The guardian ad litem has the duty to interview such persons as he thinks appropriate. These will include the foster-parents. They may be able to convince him that it is in the child's best interests to remain in their care. In any event the guardian ad litem should incorporate their views in his report to the court. In addition, the foster-parents have their own right to address the court under r. 19 (1).

Where the application to discharge the care order is *opposed* by the local authority, it is likely that the child will still have his home with his foster-parents when the application is made. They will therefore need to be notified of the application. Foster-parents are well advised to consider legal representation, even if their views directly coincide with those of the local authority. For it sometimes happens that an authority, which originally oppose discharge, revise their view in the light of the guardian ad litem's report. In these circumstances the independent right of the foster-parents to be heard could be crucial.

Where the child has been in the care of a number of persons during the relevant period it is important to determine whether all or any of such persons fall within the scope of the rule. The phrase 'a person with whom the relevant infant has had his home' has been construed in accordance with Part IV of the Children Act 1975 and the Interpretation Act 1889 to mean 'a person who has had, in the relevant period, the actual custody of the child' and that in turn means, under the CA 1975, s. 87 (1), the person who has had actual possession of the child whether or not that possession is shared with one or more other persons, *Re S (A Minor)* [1987] 1 FLR 479. This is a question of fact which must be determined at the outset of the case by the applicant in care proceedings so that all proper persons are served with notice of them. If a care order is made or discharged without proper notification being given to a person who falls within r. 14 (3) (*d*), this does not undermine the validity of the order, which stands unless and until it is quashed by a court of competent jurisdiction. However, the aggrieved person might usefully bring an application in judicial review for the court's order to be quashed and a fresh hearing to be ordered (cf. *D* v *X CC (No. 1)* [1985] FLR 275 and see §6.5.3).

7.5.4 Grandparents

A grandparent must be notified of an application brought in care proceedings if such a grandparent's whereabouts are known to the applicant or can readily be ascertained by him, CYP Rules 1988, r. 14 (3) (*c*). A grandparent is entitled to apply to be made a party to the proceedings, CYPA 1969, s. 32C and where he does the court may (not must) give him leave where it is satisfied that:

(a) the grandparent, before the commencement of the proceedings, had a substantial involvement in the infant's upbringing at any time during the infant's lifetime; and
(b) making the grandparent a party to the proceedings is likely to be in the interests of the relevant infant, r. 17 (1).

This power to make a grandparent a party is exercisable by a single justice before the hearing, CYPA 1969, s. 32 (3), or by the justices' clerk, r. 17 (2). It may also be ordered that the grandparent is given legal aid, Legal Aid Act 1974, s. 28 (6A).

A grandparent who is a party has the following rights at the hearing: to be legally represented, to give evidence, to call and cross-examine witnesses (for the order of the hearing see r. 20 (4) and §4.5.1) and to see copies of reports to the court, r. 25 (1). Where the decision is appealed the grandparent can be made a party to the appeal but cannot initiate an appeal.

It is not easy to assess how valuable these rights conferred on grandparents will prove to be in practice. For the problem remains that a juvenile court can only make or refuse to make a care or supervision order; similarly it can only discharge or refuse to discharge a care order, or substitute a supervision order. It cannot, for example, order that custody of the child be given to the grandparent. This means that even where the grandparent can persuade the court that the child's interests would best be served by the child being placed in the grandparent's care the court has no power to act on that finding. Furthermore, it may be that a court would feel inhibited from announcing any such view for courts have been expressly asked to refrain from adding any riders when making a care order (LCD Circular, JC (86) 1) (see too §7.5.6).

7.5.5 Other third parties

For those grandparents who are not made a party under r. 17 (1) and those third parties who fall outside the notification procedure of r. 14 (3) (*d*), some protection is offered by the provisions of r. 19. These entitle persons falling within r. 19 (3) to make representations to the court after the conclusion of the evidence. Such a person must satisfy the court that he has demonstrated an interest in the infant's welfare which has been maintained until the commencement of the proceedings and that his representations are likely to be of relevance to the proceedings and to the welfare of the relevant infant. Clearly the burden lies on such a person to make his interest known to the court, especially where he is not entitled to notification under r. 14. The rule could benefit, for example, foster-parents who fall outside the scope of r. 14 (3) (*d*), or relatives such as the aunt and uncle in *W* v *Hertfordshire CC* [1985] FLR 879.

7.5.6 Representations of third parties in care proceedings

Before the court can make an order, it must be satisfied both that one of the grounds for intervention has been proved *and* that the child 'is in need of care or control which he is unlikely to receive unless the court makes an order under this section in respect of him', CYPA 1969, s. 1 (2). It will not be easy to persuade a court that this latter element is missing in a case where the evidence of a parent's maltreatment of the child makes a care order the instinctive and apparently appropriate response to the application. Even if the court accepts that the love and affection offered by a grandparent or other third party makes placement with them in the child's best interests, the court is still presented with a dilemma. It can only make or refuse to make a care or supervision order. It cannot give custody to a third party. On the other hand, if it refuses to make an order, the parental rights will remain vested in the parents, and this could put the child at risk.

One solution to this dilemma is for the court to make no order on the basis that it does not have jurisdiction to make the most appropriate order in the circumstances, namely, to give custody to a third party. The court might be persuaded to adopt this solution (or alternatively simply to adjourn its proceedings), on the strict understanding that the third party will immediately make the child a ward of the High Court and apply for care and control of the child in wardship. It is suggested that this would be a proper use of wardship, namely to fill a gap in the statutory powers available to the juvenile court under the CYPA 1969, cf. *Re J (A Minor) (Wardship: Jurisdiction)* [1984] FLR 43. There would be no limit to the exercise of the High Court's jurisdiction under the principles laid down in *A* v *Liverpool CC* (1981) 2 FLR 222 and *W* v *Hertfordshire CC* [1985] FLR 879 because the child would not be in local authority care, and because a court has decided that its own powers are inadequate (see chapter 6).

Another solution would be for the court to find the application proved, but to dispose of the case by making a supervision order with a direction that the child should live with a named individual, here the third party, CYPA 1969, s. 12 (1) (see §4.7.3). This could be appropriate, particularly when the parents are content for the third party to care for the child. The difficulty is that the status of the named person is unclear, for he has neither custody of the child nor parental rights over the child.

A third but highly unlikely solution would be for the court to make a care order, but only on the understanding that the child would be placed in the care of the third party. It might go so far as to ask the local authority to give an undertaking to this effect. But this would probably be regarded as an improper attempt by a juvenile court to exercise control over a discretion given by Parliament to local authorities. Furthermore, if the local authority resiled on their undertaking there is no means by which it could be enforced by the third party. Nor would a third party have status to apply for discharge of the care order since he is neither a parent nor guardian.

As for an application to discharge a care order, here again the limitations on the court's powers make it hard for the court to respond positively to the evidence and representations of grandparents or other third parties. It cannot, for example, order that the child should remain in the care of his foster-parents or be placed in the care of his grandparents. Adjourning the case to allow the third party to commence wardship proceedings might also prove to be an inadequate response, for the local authority might object to the High Court exercising jurisdiction. However, it is suggested that it would be wrong for the High Court to apply the non-intervention principles of *A* v *Liverpool CC* (1981) 2 FLR 222 in the situation hypothesized. For where the juvenile court has clearly indicated its preferred solution the High Court should come to its aid in enabling that solution to be implemented, cf. *Re J (A Minor) (Wardship: Jurisdiction)* [1984] FLR 43.

7.6 Access Proceedings

At the time of writing, the putative father is not a parent for the purposes of Part 1A of the CCA 1980, and thus is unable to apply for access to his child in care where such access has been terminated or refused, see §5.2. It was the intention of Parliament to afford him this right by the FLRA 1987. Because of a legislative error this has not been achieved; however, the 1987 Act is to be amended in order to secure him this right. Meanwhile, although a court has jurisdiction to hear an application for access brought under the GMA 1971, s. 9, it will refuse to exercise its jurisdiction because of the principle of non-intervention in local authority decision-making, *A* v *Liverpool CC* (above) and see §6.4; *Re M and H (Minors)* [1988] 3 WLR 485.

As for other third parties, those who have the right to be notified under r. 30 may make representations under r. 30 (2). However, frequency of access is a matter for the local authority's discretion; only its termination or refusal can be litigated. This means that third parties will be able to make representations to a court only in those cases where the local authority defend their termination or refusal of access against the objection of the parent, guardian or custodian.

7.7 Foster-parents

Of all third parties special mention must be made of foster-parents. It has already been seen how they are afforded special rights of audience in the juvenile court (§7.5.3). Furthermore, as people who are caring for a child, foster-parents are often eligible to apply for an adoption or custodianship order. Where this is planned by the authority the foster-parents will normally rely on the exertions of the authority to advance their application. A detailed account of adoption and custodianship is beyond the scope of this book; but these options should be borne in mind as means of securing the long-term welfare of the child.

7.7.1 Foster-parents in conflict with the local authority

Where foster-parents are in conflict with the local authority over the authority's plans for their foster-child, their position is very weak. The authority are entitled to remove a child from his foster home at any time. If foster-parents wish to resist they can, of course, make their views known to social workers and senior management, but normally they cannot litigate the issue before a court. Unsuccessful attempts have been made to secure the intervention of the High Court in wardship, *Re M (An Infant)* [1961] Ch 328; *Re T (AJJ) (An Infant)* [1970] Ch 688; *Re DM* [1986] 2 FLR 122, the courts ruling that they will not exercise their wardship jurisdiction in an area of discretion vested by Parliament in local authorities (see §6.4). When foster-parents have cared for a child for several years they may be determined to resist removal of their foster-child (see the facts of *Re H (A Minor) (Adoption)* [1985] FLR 519). Two options are open to them.

7.7.2 Remedy of Adoption

An adoption application by foster-parents does not automatically prevent the removal of the child from their care by the local authority, but they will be protected in two situations. First, where an application is made by persons with whom the child has had his home for the preceding five years, no person is entitled to remove the child from the applicants' home while the application is pending, Adoption Act 1976 (AA), s. 28 (1). Secondly, foster-parents can obtain protection from an earlier date by giving notice in writing to the local authority that they intend to apply for an adoption order. For where the child has had his home with them for the preceding five years, no person can remove the child from them before they apply for the adoption order, or before a period of three months from the receipt of the notice by the local authority expires, whichever occurs first, s. 28 (2). Both provisions afford the prospective adopters protection against removal of the child even by the local authority and despite the fact that the child is in care, s. 28 (3). However, where reliance is placed on s. 28 (2) the prospective adopters must put in their adoption application within three months or they will lose their protection against the child's removal, as a fresh notice of intention to adopt cannot be issued until 28 days have elapsed after the expiry of the original notice, s. 28 (6).

   In *Re H (A Minor) (Adoption)* [1985] FLR 519 it was held following *A* v *Liverpool CC* (1981) 2 FLR 222 that where the purpose of an adoption application is to frustrate the local authority in their choice of a fostering placement, the court ought not to exercise its discretion under the adoption legislation for the purpose of overruling an intended exercise by the authority of their powers under the CCA 1980. It is suggested, however, that it is inappropriate for courts to approach adoption applications applying the principles laid down in *A* v *Liverpool CC* (above) and *W* v *Hertfordshire CC* [1985] FLR 879 (see chapter 6). For in these circumstances there are no constitutional reasons for denying the courts a judicial role, and adoption legislation contemplates cases where applications will be made without the support of the local authority. The approach taken in *Re H* (above) fails to take account of s. 28 of the AA 1976 which specifically permits an application for adoption to be made despite opposition from the local authority. Furthermore, in reaching any decision relating to the adoption of a child, a court must give first consideration to the need to safeguard and promote the welfare of the child throughout his childhood, AA 1976, s. 6. Thus the decision-making function is firmly given to the court and not the local authority.

7.7.3 Custodianship

Foster-parents would normally be better advised to apply for a custodianship order. The effect of an order is to leave the legal status of the child intact, but to give legal custody of the child to the applicants. The persons qualified to apply for an order are:

- (a) a relative or step-parent of the child –
  - (i) who applies with the consent of a person having legal custody of the child, and
  - (ii) with whom the child has had his home for three months preceding the making of the application;
- (b) any person –
  - (i) who applies with the consent of a person having legal custody of the child, and
  - (ii) with whom the child has had his home for a period or periods before the making of the application which amount to at least twelve months and include the three months preceding the making of the application;
- (c) any person with whom the child has had his home for a period or periods before the making of the application which amount to at least three years and include the three months preceding the application, Children Act 1975, s. 33 (3).

Consent is needed from a person with legal custody. Where the child is in care under s. 2 of the CCA 1980, foster-parents who wish to apply for a custodianship order in respect of a child boarded out with them should obtain the consent of one of the child's parents. The consent of the authority is not needed before an application is made. However, where the local authority have assumed parental rights under s. 3 of the CCA 1980, or where there is a care order, a custodianship application can only be made with the consent of the authority, unless the child has had his home with the applicants for more than three years. The authority cannot defeat an application without consent made after three years simply by removing the child from the applicants. For, provided the application is pending, no person, including a local authority, is entitled to remove the child from the applicants' custody except with the leave of the court, Children Act 1975, s. 41.

In *Re H (A Minor) (Adoption)* [1985] FLR 519 a boy aged eleven and a girl aged nine had been living with the same foster-parents for the last seven years. The local authority told them that they intended to remove the boy to another foster placement. The foster-parents realized that if the boy went it was likely that the girl would be moved too. The children were having regular access to their father, and the foster-parents' application to adopt them was refused. *Re H* preceded the implementation of custodianship, but Sir John Arnold P commented:

'If ever there was a case which cried out for a consideration of the custodianship provisions of the Children Act 1975 this is that case. . . . I do not wish to say that this is a case in which custodianship would certainly be the order of the court, but it seems at least likely that the preservation of the children in the household of the foster-parents would have been usefully assured by a dependence on these provisions.'

Significantly the court implicitly accepted that an application for custodianship could properly be made by foster-parents in conflict with a local authority, even though the same court had disapproved of an adoption application being made to defeat the local authority.

It may be that, where a local authority intend to remove a child from long-term foster-parents without their agreement, the authority should give them the opportunity to apply for custodianship. A failure to do so might then be challengeable by judicial review, cf. *Re M (Minors)* (1986) LSG 780. Alternatively, where the local authority appear to have acted unreasonably and irrationally and against the near unanimous opposition of those with direct knowledge of the child, judicial review might be available, see the *obiter dicta* in *Re H (A Minor) (Adoption)* (above) and §6.5.

7.8 Conclusion

Litigation should normally be seen as the last resort in child-care cases, for it is not conducive to conserving human relationships or to the proper management of matters in the future. Where there is intransigence from the social workers primarily responsible for a case, it may be that the authority can employ their own internal grievance procedures. These are designed to accommodate aggrieved parents, but may be sufficiently flexible to allow a third party a hearing. Sensitive discussion and conciliation on behalf of a client is more likely to lead to an acceptable outcome than an open confrontation, and is more likely to promote the welfare of the child, which should be the primary goal of all who are concerned in child-care cases.

INDEX